MACKENZIE KING
His Life and World

CP–1

FRONTISPIECE William Lyon
Mackenzie King by Sir
William Orpen. This
portrait hangs near the
entrance to Laurier House.
*Laurier House, Public
Archives Canada.*

J. L. GRANATSTEIN
MACKENZIE KING
His Life and World

General Editor: W. Kaye Lamb

Picture Editor: Paul Russell

McGraw-Hill Ryerson Limited

Toronto   Montreal   New York   London

ISBN 0-07-082304-9

1 2 3 4 5 6 7 8 9 10 BP 6 5 4 3 2 1 0 9 8 7

Printed and bound in Canada

For Michael

Canadian Cataloguing in Publication Data

Granatstein, J. L., 1939–
   Mackenzie King: his life and world

Bibliography: p.
Includes index.
ISBN 0-07-082304-9

1. King, William Lyon Mackenzie, 1874-1950.
2. Prime ministers — Canada — Biography. 3. Canada —
Politics and government — 1911-   *   I. Title.

FC581.K5G73   971.06′32′0924   C77-001142-X
F1033.K53G73

TITLE PAGE Mono-
gram and signature
of William Lyon
Mackenzie King.
*Public Archives
Canada, C-46507
and C-46508.*

087162

Contents

1
King and Canada, 1919

"THIS TO BE A YEAR of momentous decisions so far as my own life is concerned." With those words, Mackenzie King began his diary on New Year's Day, 1919. He was right. Before the year was out, King would be elected leader of the Liberal Party, the heir of Sir Wilfrid Laurier at the head of one of the two political parties of the Dominion. For an ambitious man whose longstanding goal had been to be the Prime Minister of Canada, this was a substantial advance. Given the state of the country, the unrest, the inflation, the widespread disillusionment with the Union government of Sir Robert Borden, to be leader of the Liberal party was virtually to be guaranteed success in the next general election.

Mackenzie King was not the most likely of political leaders. At the beginning of this first year of peace following World War I, he was 44 years old, a bachelor, and a short, fresh-faced man looking much younger than his years. His mother, a daughter of William Lyon Mackenzie, the rebel of 1837, had controlled and shaped her son's growth and development, filling him with a zeal to restore his grandfather's reputation and stature together with an intense desire to fulfill mama's expectations. Mrs. King dominated her son's life to an unfortunate, almost unhealthy degree, a condition of affairs that her death in 1917 scarcely altered. That King remained a bachelor could be attributed to his mother's influence; that King considered himself a reformer could almost certainly be attributed to her.

The reforming streak had come to the fore even while King was a student. Toronto, Chicago, and Boston all had their share of prostitution, and the young King devoted a fair amount of his time to persuade these wayward girls and women

7

Mackenzie King in 1876, riding his
rocking horse at the age of two.
Public Archives Canada, C-14189.

to give up their sinful life. This "rescue work," not at all dissimilar to that which William Ewart Gladstone, the British Prime Minister and one of King's political heroes, had undertaken 40 years earlier, clearly posed problems for King. It was God's work to reform these females, but there was also temptation in it. There is no incontrovertible evidence that King ever succumbed, but there can be no doubt that he was sorely tempted on many occasions, or that he was ashamed of the conflicting emotions that wrestled within him. He was a frustrated man, tortured by sex, and he would remain so.*

Although he had no record of outstanding political success behind him, King did represent almost the archetype of the "promising young man." He had been educated at the University of Toronto, the University of Chicago, and Harvard, from which he received a doctorate in economics. He had built for himself a standing as a sociologist and as an expert in labour relations, and with a little help from his friends he had transformed this reputation into the position of Deputy Minister in the newly formed Department of Labour in Ottawa in 1900. For a young man of 26, this was a start at the top, and for the next eight years King held this civil service post, founding and editing the *Labour Gazette*, the government's record of labour conditions, strikes and industrial relations, and drafting legislation for his Minister. Occasionally, too, King went abroad on missions, for investigations, and above all for the opportunity of meeting the great and famous. Contacts once made were never allowed to lapse.

*For a very different interpretation of King's sexuality, see Col. Charles Stacey, *A Very Double Life* (Toronto, 1976). The parallel with Gladstone is instructive. H. C. G. Matthew, the editor of *The Gladstone Diaries*, writes at some length on Gladstone's sexual difficulties, always sympathetically and never in a voyeuristic manner. "Priggish and hypocritical he may have seemed to enemies," Matthew noted in words that could easily have been applied to Mackenzie King, "foolhardy to friends, but his struggles with his body and his conscience, when seen in the diary in the context of his religious, political and family life, cannot but seem noble." Matthew adds, "It is tempting to see Gladstone, because of his religious and political prominence, as exceptional in these matters, but perhaps if more middle-class Victorians had recorded their secret lives so assiduously and honestly he would not seem so; indeed he might seem, rather than a curiousity, predominantly an abstainant." (M. R. D. Foot and H. C. G. Matthew, *The Gladstone Diaries*, Vol. III: 1840-47 [Oxford, 1974], pp. xlv-xlviii.) Substitute "King" for "Gladstone" in that last sentence, and much of Mackenzie King's life, his double life, is put into proper focus.

Mackenzie King's mother, Mrs. Isabel Grace (Mackenzie) King. A portrait by Lyonde of Toronto. *Public Archives Canada, C-46524.*

The young King made the leap to active politics in 1908 when he ran for the Liberals in Waterloo North, Ontario, his home area, and he won the seat. In June 1909, Prime Minister Laurier took him into the cabinet as Minister of Labour, when he was still on the near side of 35. As Minister, he was active and indefatigable, always in the public eye and efficient, but not a first-rank member of the party's gray-bearded frontbench in the House of Commons. Still, people looked on him as a man to watch, a comer, and in his own mind at least Mackenzie King convinced himself that he was destined to succeed Laurier, indeed that he was Laurier's chosen successor.

There would be difficult years between that wish and its realization. The Liberals went down to defeat in the reciprocity election in 1911 and Mackenzie King lost his seat. The next years were hard ones for Liberalism and for Canada, made more so by the decline in economic conditions after 1911 and by the Great War that began in 1914. Sir Robert Borden's

An older Mrs. King. One of Mackenzie
King's favourite portraits. Painting by
Frank O. Salisbury.
Courtesy of Mrs. Jean Dunlop.

Conservative government committed Canada heart and soul to the war, and the national contribution grew by leaps and bounds. By the thousands men were trained, equipped, and despatched overseas to the slaughterhouse that was France and Flanders; by the thousands they were swallowed up as the war destroyed "the flower of Canadian youth" in battles for worthless yards of muddy ground. At home the war also destroyed relations between French and English Canadians and ruined both the Liberal and Conservative parties.

The issue was conscription. Fresh recruits were in short supply by the beginning of 1917. In May Sir Robert Borden returned to Canada from the United Kingdom, convinced that only compulsion could secure enough men to keep the four Canadian divisions up to strength. Sir Wilfrid Laurier could not agree. The old chief believed that the voluntary system had never been employed to its fullest extent and certainly not in Quebec. He feared that conscription would drive a permanent wedge between his compatriots and the English speaking: he was probably convinced that, though the war was important, it was not so important — nothing could be so important — as to justify tearing the country apart for the sake of a few more men. Certainly conscription split the country as English Canadians pressed for its imposition while French Canadians resisted it mightily. Conscription, Quebec believed, would be acceptable in a war to defend Canada; in no way could it be considered in a European war; in no way could it be tolerated when English Canadians viewed it as another way of forcing the humiliation of the Conquest of 1759 on Quebec once more. Far-fetched and strained? Perhaps, but most Canadians did perceive England's war as Canada's own and many thought the fractious French had to be taught a lesson and made to assume their share of sacrifice.

This racial split in the nation was reproduced in the Liberal party. English-speaking Liberals, many of whom had stood with Laurier for decades and who dearly loved their leader, broke relations and deserted their party. Only French Canadians and a few hardy souls in the English-speaking provinces stood with the old man. One such was Mackenzie King, a man who did not oppose conscription as much as he esteemed party loyalty. His loyalist position in 1917 would be one of the great selling points to Quebec that he would employ at the Liberal leadership convention of 1919 — and ever after.

The Liberal split led directly to the formation of a Union government under Borden in the fall of 1917. The govern-

OPPOSITE Mackenzie King, age 14, photographed in 1888 with his parents and his elder sister, Bella. King had a brother and two sisters.
Public Archives Canada, C-7348.

13

King in cap and gown on his 17th birthday in December 1891, shortly after he became a student at the University of Toronto. He graduated, with first-class honours, in 1895. *Public Archives Canada, C-2853.*

ment that fought and won the bitter December election of that year and imposed conscription was almost wholly English-speaking. It was a government bound together only by concern for the needs of the trenches, and it had no common ground on other issues. Some of its members were traditional Conservative high-tariff proponents; others were Prairie farmers whose entire careers had been bound up in a crusade for free trade. Nothing held this government together beyond its concern to bring the war to a victorious close.

At times this overriding concern for the needs of the war threatened to bring the country close to civil war. At Easter

In 1900, when he became Deputy
Minister of Labour, King invited his
friend Bert Harper to become his
assistant. Sadly, however, Harper
drowned in 1901 while trying to
rescue a woman from the Ottawa
River. King pressed his cabinet contacts for a memorial to Harper's
gallantry, and in 1905 the result was
unveiled on Parliament Hill — a
statue, *Sir Galahad*.
Parks Canada.

1918, the streets of Quebec City were full of rioters protesting the enforcement of the Military Service Act, the conscription bill. This unrest was squelched when troops were brought in — including an Ontario regiment. Quebeckers were not the only ones upset by the Military Service Act. Already politically restive, farmers had been promised exemption from the draft for their sons by the Minister of Militia and Defence two weeks before the election of 1917, and the rural voters had responded appropriately at the polls. But with the great German offensive of the spring of 1918, with the threat of defeat staring the Allies in the face, the government rescinded all exemptions and cancelled its election promises. The farmers' protests were to no avail, and yet another segment of the population had additional grievances to store up for the peace.

The armistice on November 11, 1918, began the dissolution of the Borden government. The country faced terrible problems that the afterglow of victory could not long conceal. This nation of just over 8 million had sustained a massive war

Mackenzie King in 1900, looking very youthful at the age of 26, when he joined the civil service as first editor of the *Labour Gazette*. Within a few months he advanced to the rank of Deputy Minister of Labour. Just before starting up the *Gazette*, he had spent ten months studying and travelling in Europe. While abroad he experimented with a moustache and beard, but he discarded both and remained clean shaven ever after. *Public Archives Canada, PA-25941.*

An informal picture of Mackenzie King in 1910, age 36, when he was Minister of Labour in the Laurier government. A separate Department of Labour, with its own minister, had been created in 1909; King was the first to hold the portfolio. *Public Archives Canada, PA-25970.*

effort for more than four years. As its result there were more than 60,000 dead, 173,000 suffering from wounds or injuries, including 11,500 wasting away from the effects of poison gas. The costs had been terrible in human terms; they were dear in monetary terms too. Then there was the necessity to integrate the returned men into society once more, to offer them jobs and understanding, to offer the rewards that a grateful nation owed those who had risked everything. That had to be the first charge on the state.

That charge would not be met. The coming of the peace disrupted the booming factories of Canada. Munitions plants, vital to the war effort on November 10, were superfluous the next day. Jobs began to dry up while living costs continued

Mackenzie King speaking at a Liberal demonstration in Simcoe, Ontario, shortly before the 1911 general election in which he was defeated.
Public Archives Canada, C-46311.

to mount. The cost-of-living index (based on a scale of 1935-39 equalling 100) had risen from 80.0 in 1914 to 104.3 in 1917 to 118.1 in 1918. When peace came, the index accelerated dramatically to 129.8 in 1919 to 150.5 in 1920. Wage rates rose as well, but with the surplus of labour brought by the peace there were always men willing to take work for whatever wage they could get. Many soldiers, expecting a hero's welcome, were shattered to find themselves on the dole or living uneasily off their demobilization allowances.

Those workers with jobs were unhappy too. The inflated prices for food and clothing left them short every payday; many workers found themselves forced into unions as their only hope for a fair wage. Employers resisted, of course, and strikes followed. Some of the labour unrest was motivated by revolutionary intentions, as militants hoped to emulate the Great Russian Revolution in Canada. But most of it sprang directly out of need, as did the Winnipeg General Strike of 1919 that tied up the city for weeks in May and June that year. The strike was crushed by the intervention of the federal government's police and military power as well as by the mobilization of the "good" citizens of the town. But other strikes continued throughout the land, and as prices rose tension increased.

At this juncture the Liberals met in convention at Ottawa in August, a gathering made necessary by the death of Laurier in February 1919. This meeting, the first national leadership convention held by either of the two major parties, brought together more than 1200 Liberal delegates from all the provinces. The tenor of the meeting was optimistic about the party's prospects, but there were hard feelings still about those Liberals who had deserted Laurier and this showed in the selection of the leader.

The leading contender for Laurier's mantle was W. S. Fielding, the longtime Minister of Finance in the Laurier administrations and before that a Premier of Nova Scotia. In terms of service and ability Fielding was probably entitled to the post, but he had been a reluctant Unionist in 1917 and after, an alliance which seemed an insuperable barrier to many Laurier loyalists. He was also a staunch high-tariff man: in some parts of the country that too seemed a heresy. Besides, Fielding was 70 years old. Was 1919 the time for a septuagenarian? delegates wondered.

Mackenzie King with John D. Rockefeller, Jr. (at right), and Archie Dennison, a miner, in Colorado in 1915. King was studying industrial relations (and in particular the problems of Rockefeller's Colorado Fuel and Iron Company) under the auspices of the Rockefeller Foundation.
Public Archives Canada, C-29350.

There were two additional candidates for the leadership. One was George P. Graham of Ontario, 60 years of age, a former Minister of Railways and Canals from 1907 to 1911; D. D. McKenzie, a lacklustre Nova Scotian, was the other. He had been in the House of Commons since 1904, and had been selected as interim leader by the Liberal caucus after Laurier's death. If McKenzie is remembered at all today, it is because a French-speaking MP, when asked why McKenzie had been chosen House leader, replied, "He will always remind us of Laurier. He is so different." Neither Graham nor McKenzie was a strong entry into the race.

The final candidate, of course, was Mackenzie King. A dark horse and the youngest of the contenders by far at 44, King seemed to be a break from the past and its defeats and tensions. He also seemed a man for the times, for he was well qualified to deal with labour questions, the key issue of the moment. Indeed, he had written a book, *Industry and Humanity*, published the year before, that expressed his fervent views on the need for industrialists to deal humanely with labour. Written in convoluted prose, high-falutin' in places, obscure in most, his book was enlivened not at all by diagrams that sketched King's view of the cosmos. But for all that, the book was there, and its very presence tended to mark King as an expert. His earlier efforts in the United States, where he had worked on industrial conciliation prior to and early in the war for John D. Rockefeller, Jr. — unkind critics charged that he had set up company unions — also inspired confidence that King was the right man to deal with the labour crisis of the hour. In addition to these powerful arguments in his favour, King was acceptable to French Canada and to Quebec's delegates, none of whom was allowed to forget that he had stood with Laurier in 1917.

The convention rules did not permit the candidates to address the delegates formally. But each had the opportunity to speak during the discussion of party platform resolutions, and Mackenzie King, naturally enough, chose to address the delegates on labour and industry. Not only was this King's area of expertise, but he had also chaired the convention's preliminary platform committee on labour and industry. Under his lead the Liberals adopted a program that included support for the living wage, the eight-hour day, unemployment insurance, old-age pensions, and mother's allowances. It was a progressive statement and, as King said later, it was "a

1—9
OPPOSITE Photographs of Laurier and King together, such as this one taken in August 1915, are rare. The woman is not identified. *Public Archives Canada,* C-46319.

chart on which is plotted the course desired by the people of the country."

The candidate's speech was remarkably effective as he spoke of his resolutions. Contrary to popular memory today, King could deliver a rousing speech, and on this critical occasion he rose to the challenge. There was the graceful tribute to Laurier, the late leader who had fought and died "for the right of the people to control the Parliament of their country" and a devastating assault on the record of failures achieved by the Borden government. When he finished, the delegates stood up and cheered him to the echo. Many delegates had come to Ottawa undecided and unsure of their choice for leader; after King's speech, the options were clearer, for his appeal seemed easily the most able and attractive delivered by the candidates.

On the first ballot King received 344 votes to Fielding's 297, while Graham and McKenzie won 153 each. Because the last two were tied, both stayed in the race for the second ballot which King again led with 411 votes, followed by Fielding with 344, Graham with 124, and only 60 for McKenzie. The third ballot ended the contest and, with Graham and McKenzie both now having retired, King won narrowly with 476 votes to Fielding's 438. King had captured the leadership of the party in one of the great upsets in Canadian political history, and he won because Quebec stood with him. Sir Allen Aylesworth, Laurier's old Ontario lieutenant and a King supporter, summed up the decisive nature of the French-Canadian support in a letter to his brother:

> You never saw such friends as those Frenchmen are to stick to a man they like. Dozens of them *hugged* me. They'd have kissed me if I would let them — and they voted — every man Jack of them — just to stand by the men who had stood by Laurier. That is the whole story in a nutshell — let the newspapers prattle all they like.

The loyalty and devotion of the French Canadians to one they trusted had won the Liberal leadership for King. That was a lesson he would never forget.

2
The Politics of Reconciliation

THE LIBERAL PARTY that Mackenzie King surveyed after the convention of 1919 was divided and torn by dissension. Part of this dissension, the grumbling of supporters of the defeated candidates, would disappear in due course. More serious by far were the deeper structural cracks in party unity. Only French Canadians seemed firmly attached to the Liberal party, and that was more a knee-jerk response to Laurier's memory than a commitment to party policy. And what was that party policy? Despite the convention platform, who knew? The Liberals under Laurier had been a progressive-conservative party, in general supporting the national tariff, in general devoted to developing the nation's resources, in general a party that worked closely with business interests and that had ridden the crest of the economic boom of the first decade of this century. French Canada was conservative at heart, it seemed; Laurier's policies had appealed to this close-to-the-vest attitude.

The Western Liberals, however, would have none of this. At their urging, Laurier had turned to the support of reciprocity in 1911 and gone to defeat; against their pleas Laurier had resisted conscription in 1917. The West had turned to the Union government in the general election that year, an election that essentially helped destroy the established party machines in the Prairie provinces. The Liberal provincial organizations had broken ranks and turned *en bloc* to the Unionist party; the Conservative organizations, never very strong in the West, had been effectively smashed by the resentment about the removal of conscription exemptions in the spring of 1918. The West was a political vacuum ready for change.

As always, Ontario remained the crucial area for federal

politicians. Rich, powerful, aggressive, it dominated Confederation and imposed its will on national politicians. And
Ontario's will was for more protection for its factories and
for an easy climate at Ottawa in which business could operate
untrammelled and unfettered. Since the beginning of the century, Ontario voters had been becoming more Tory in their
voting; in the elections of 1911 and 1917 the Liberals had been
decimated at the polls. This trend would have to alter if Mackenzie King were to succeed.

In the Maritimes the Liberals were in fair shape. The
Atlantic provinces had their own deep loyalties that tended to
protect them from the buffeting winds of public opinion, and
in 1917 they had given Laurier ten seats, half of the Liberal
total outside Quebec. Here at least was a base on which to build.

How to proceed? This was the problem that Mackenzie
King faced as the 1920s began. One point was immediately
evident. The Liberal party had to operate in such a way that
it would be a home for everyone; it had to be a genuine omni-

bus party travelling down the centre of the political road. There could be no permanent barriers to those who had lapsed into Unionism in 1917; there could be no barriers to those who favoured a high tariff or a low one; there could be no barriers to the representatives of capital or labour. Everyone who opposed the past and present policies of Borden's government could stand with the Liberals. Everyone could go forward with Mackenzie King.

This was not a particularly principled position, but it was one in line with that adopted by successful Canadian political leaders in the past. Principles were good things and every man and woman had to have them, but politics required understanding, conciliation, and compromise. The important thing was to get the party back together to create a national organization that brought together representatives from all parts of the nation, from all classes, from all races. This togetherness had to be King's goal in the first years of his leadership; it would still be his goal when he left politics almost thirty years later.

The problem faced by King was that the differentiation between classes was as sharp as it ever had been in Canada. Inflation hurt everyone on a fixed salary, while stock profiteers, industrialists, and other speculators grew richer than ever. Farmers, hurt by rising costs for the goods they needed, could at least raise the prices they charged for their produce, but the worker in the cities — and Canada in 1921 had an even distribution of population in the country and the cities — had only strictly limited options and tended to focus discontent on the profiteering farmers. The whole atmosphere of unrest in the world typified by the Russian civil war that pitted the "people" against the representatives of the "oligarchy" added to the uneasiness. Joseph Flavelle, the meat-packing baron and financier who had served during the war as the head of the Imperial Munitions Board, wrote to a friend to bemoan the results of the 1919 election in Ontario, where a farmer's government was elected:

> . . . we have apparently . . . in matters generally political, established a class consciousness which leads men to seek election to Parliament as representatives of a class in support of class legislation. It is interesting to note that the two classes in the community, viz. Agriculturalists and Labor, who have peculiarly prospered during the war . . . are the classes who claim particular representation in Parliament for their own class.

ABOVE Thomas A. Crerar, a key figure in the vigorous but short-lived farmers' political movement that resulted in the election of 64 Progressives to Parliament in 1921 — more than double the representation any other third party has ever had in the House of Commons. *Public Archives of Canada, PA-43102.*

OPPOSITE The Rt. Hon. Arthur Meighen, a brilliant debater and one of the ablest men ever to sit in the Canadian Parliament. He despised Mackenzie King, who in turn both disliked and feared him; however, in the long run Meighen proved to be no match for King in politics. *Public Archives Canada, C-5799.*

29

For Flavelle and others like him who had been used to having their particular and general interests represented in Parliament and satisfied there, this was an unhappy state of affairs.

Unsatisfactory or not, class politics seemed to be the wave of the future. The rural dwellers of Ontario were only the first to rise up in revolt, joined by many members of the working classes in the cities of the industrial south. The philosophy of the day was group politics, and the organized farm associations were its chief proponent. "Why enter politics as a group?" asked William Irvine, a Presbyterian clergyman who had been caught up in the ferment of ideas in the Prairies during and after the war:

> The United Farmers are taking political action as a group . . . because they are convinced that party politics is corrupt and inefficient. . . . The farmers think that to get rid of partyism you must get rid of the party idea altogether. . . . The farmers have been voting for party candidates ever since Confederation, but they have never had representation; their industry has been ignored by legislators, and the voice of their opinion has been drowned in the party cry.

Parties had to go. Group government — a government in which each class and major economic interest in the community would be represented — was the answer, because in such a system the selfishness of one group would be checked by the self-interest of the others. In Canadian party politics, the farmers argued convincingly, only the interests of the manufacturers and profiteers were served.

It is unlikely that the farmers as a whole understood the theory their leaders were articulating. But their unhappiness with the old party system was clear. Jimmy Gardiner, in 1921 as Saskatchewan MLA who would become the Premier of the province and later King's Agriculture Minister, recalled that he had talked with an old German farmer when he was campaigning for Mackenzie King that year. "I voted Liberal in 1911 and the Liberal MP changed to Union Government in 1917," he said. "How do I know that if I vote Liberal this time the MP will stay Liberal?" That was a good question and one that summed up the rural disillusionment with the old parties. Some way had to be discovered to ensure that Members of Parliament did not act against the interests of those who had elected them and sent them to Ottawa. The Western farmers pondered these questions and concluded that their candidates should leave signed but undated resignations with their constituencies, for use when and if needed. They gave thought to ways in which the legislation-making process could become more democratic; they explored the use of the initiative and the referendum as devices. The Western farmers' whole intent was to open up the process of government, to demystify it, and to make sure that promises once made by politicians were implemented.

The best safeguard, of course, seemed to be to elect farmers to Parliament. Farmers would act in their constituents' interests, and the result was the loosely organized Progressive party under the nominal leadership of Thomas Crerar, a Manitoba farmer who had become President of the Grain Growers' Grain Company and the Minister of Agriculture in the Union government of 1917. Crerar had stuck with Borden until the war was won, but the coming of peace pointed up the contradictions between his views and those of the government, and he had resigned in June 1919. Like many of the Unionists of 1917 in the West, Crerar had been a Liberal and would be again. But in the initial years after the war, he was fed up to the teeth with both the old parties, and he almost automatically assumed the leadership of the new farmers' movement.

However, Crerar was not convinced of the efficacy of the group-government approach. After all, he had spent some time in Parliament, and he knew the resiliency of the party system and the difficulties inherent in trying to alter it branch and root. Crerar was more of a gradualist than some of his nominal followers, particularly those in the United Farmers of Alberta, so he was willing to settle for good legislation of value to his people. In some eyes that was almost treason, but as the election of December 1921 approached, those divisions in the ranks of the Progressives were not yet evident.

The Union government too would enter the political combat under new leadership and with a new name. In the summer of 1920, the Unionist caucus met and agreed that henceforth the party would answer to the unwieldy handle of "The National Liberal and Conservative Party," a name chosen in an obvious effort to hold the Unionist Liberals. At the same time, Arthur Meighen became leader of the party and Prime Minister, succeeding Sir Robert Borden who had been in bad health for months. Unlike Mackenzie King, Meighen was not chosen by a national convention but by Borden alone after difficult and lengthy negotiations with the cabinet and caucus. The caucus was heavily for Meighen, but

RIGHT A pension landmark: Mr. A. W. Neill, MP for Comox-Alberni, presenting the first Old Age Pension cheque to William Henry Derby, of Alberni. The cheque, dated September 20, 1927, was never cashed, as Mr. Neill, long an advocate of the pension scheme, purchased it from Mr. Derby and retained it as a souvenir. It is now in the Public Archives of Canada. British Columbia was the first province to implement the joint pension program with the federal government. Mr. R. J. Burde, MLA, who sponsored the enabling legislation in the provincial legislature, stands next to Mr. Neill.
Howard H. Ward Collection, Public Archives of Canada, C-21247.

2—4a
BELOW *Canadian Annual Review, 1927-28. Metropolitan Toronto Library Board.*

Left to right—W. H. Derby; A. W. Neill, M.P., Comox-Alberni; R. J. Burde, M.L.A., Alberni; A. G. Freeze, Government Agent, Alberni.

Some Events of the Year.

Under an Order-in-Council signed at 'Ottawa on Sept. 29, 1927, an agreement under which British Columbia undertook to put into effect Old Age Pension legislation passed by the Dominion Parliament, became operative and on Oct. 15 the first cheques were issued, being retroactive to Sept. 1. Administration was in the hands of the Workmen's Compensation Board and British Columbia was the first Province to adopt the system.

the ministers were almost unanimously opposed to him, preferring instead Sir Thomas White, the Minister of Finance. White, however, was unwilling to serve because of ill health, and Borden eventually persuaded his colleagues to accept Meighen. It was not a particularly auspicious beginning.

The new Prime Minister was a man of formidable qualities. He was probably the best debater in the House of Commons, the most prodigious worker, and possibly the best intellect. Meighen was born in 1874, the same year as Mackenzie King, and like him attended the University of Toronto, taking a degree in mathematics. After a fling at teaching, he moved west to Manitoba where he was called to the bar. First elected to Parliament in 1908, he quickly made a mark with his oratorical skill, and Borden named him Solicitor General in 1913. With the coming of the war his responsibilities mounted, and he soon became the man that Borden turned to to solve all the hot problems facing the government. Meighen largely drafted the Military Service Act of 1917; Meighen shaped the Wartime Elections Act that so greatly aided the Unionist victory by disfranchising the "disloyal" and enfranchising the female relatives of soldiers; Meighen also went to Winnipeg in 1919 to put down the General Strike. He was able, but his ability had saddled him with a reputation that would be difficult to overcome. To French Canadians, he was a bloody-handed monster; to immigrant groups, he was responsible for stealing their votes away; to labour, he was a strikebreaker. Ironically, because Meighen had supported the government's railway-nationalization proposals during and after the war, the business interests of Montreal hated him vehemently. The "mathematician in politics," as the Tory propagandists called him, had "achieved the summit of political eminence by the sheer force of his intellect," but he would hold that summit only for the briefest of periods.

Meighen's past was an electoral liability in parts of the nation, but his present helped him not at all. The postwar inflation had galloped through 1919 and 1920, but the crushing deflation that began in 1921 hurt almost as much. Unemployment mounted until more than 20 per cent of the union members in Montreal were jobless, until 10,000 were out of work in Vancouver and there were long queues for meal tickets. Canada as yet had no unemployment insurance, so private welfare had to fill the void. It tried, but it could not hope to succeed: many suffered real privation. The deflation also saw a tightening of credit, and this tight-money situation hit par-

Bourgeois, 1926   *La Presse, Montreal*

KING — Je vous rends la clef de ma chambre, je compte revenir au mois d'août.

Bourgeois, cartoonist for *La Presse*, Montreal, depicts Mr. King checking out of the Hôtel du Canada in June 1926, but confident that he will be back in August. (Actually the general election was not held until September.) *Metropolitan Toronto Library Board*.

ticularly hard at farmers, already badly battered by the decline in wheat prices from wartime peaks of $2.24 a bushel for No. 1 Northern in 1918 to $1.99 in 1920 and to $1.29 in 1921. The economic downturn increased the farmers' unhappiness; the decline in the cost of living did little for the thousands unable to secure work.

The Prime Minister was not unaware of these problems. How could he be? His campaign, nonetheless, hinged around the protective tariff. "I stand for a protective tariff," Meighen stated baldly, "and I have always done so." The tariff question should have had appeal in Quebec, traditionally a part of the country that had benefited from it. But in Quebec Meighen was hurt by his conscriptionist past, a liability that he faced in a characteristically forthright manner. "I never try to ride two horses," the Prime Minister told a Quebec audience. "I fa-

voured conscription. I introduced the Military Service Act. . . .
I did because I thought it was right." That was admirable, but
it was not politics, and the tariff seemed a safer line to furrow.
The first issue of the *National Liberal and Conservative Bul-
letin*, released six months before the election as the government began to ready its campaign ammunition, spelled it out:
"Keep Canadian Markets for Canadian Products." Again and
again the Conservative leader played on this theme, arguing
that the tariff was necessary if Canadian workers were to have
jobs and Canadian manufacturing were to thrive. "If I can but
get the people in this country to see that the issue is Protection
or no Protection," he said, "the battle will be won."

Unfortunately for Meighen and the Conservatives, the
people could see it all too clearly, particularly people in the
West. There, Tom Crerar preached the need for the lowest
tariff possible and for reciprocity with the United States, and
this message was widely accepted by farmers anxious to get
cheap farm implements and manufactured goods and not
caring very much where they came from.

Mackenzie King's position was less clear than that of
either of his opponents. In the first place, his party had tariff
partisans and opponents: depending on where he spoke, King
seemed to wax enthusiastic or lukewarm on the virtues of protection. In addition, to King the Progressives seemed merely
disgruntled Liberals who would soon find a congenial home
back in the party. This waffling demanded caution from the
leader, even though many Ontario and Quebec Liberals believed the tariff to be the key issue.

In such circumstances, King tried to talk about other
issues as much as he could. "In the mind of the Prime Minister,"
he said, the tariff may be the issue; "in the mind of the people,
the issue is the Prime Minister himself and what he and his
colleagues represent of autocracy and extravagance in the management of public affairs." Meighen's government was the government of the Wartime Elections Act, the government by
order in council, the government of high taxes, the government
that had brought high costs and unemployment. In his speeches,
Mackenzie King could be very clear in attacking the government but opaque and oblique when indicating his own views,
always preferring the hedged phrase over the clear and forthright statement. The contrast with Meighen could not have
been more sharp, but King did not worry too much about it.
"I have gone through the campaign without saying one unkind
or harsh expression I am aware of, and without being irritated

36

at any point. . . . I don't think I have made enemies, and I know I have made hosts of friends." Arthur Meighen could not claim that.

The election results revealed the great regional, racial, and economic divisions in the country. The Prairies voted heavily for the Progressives, giving the farmers' party 37 seats, leaving the Conservatives without a seat from the Ontario border to British Columbia, and giving Mackenzie King only two constituencies. In Saskatchewan the Progressives took 61 per cent of the popular vote, in Alberta 52.5 per cent. Prime Minister Meighen lost his own seat in Portage la Prairie to a Progressive candidate. The results in Quebec were just as disheartening for the Tories, as King swept every one of the province's 65 seats and over 70 per cent of the popular vote. Only in British Columbia (where they won 7 of 13), in the Yukon (where they took the only seat), in New Brunswick (where they captured 5 of the 11 seats) and in Ontario (where they took 37 of 82 seats) did the Conservatives survive. The Progressives also won 24 seats in Ontario, three more than the Liberals. The results, then, had Meighen's Conservatives reduced to 50 seats, a loss of 103 from the great Unionist sweep of 1917. The Progressives ended up with 64, while Mackenzie King had 116. With five independents in a House of Commons of 235 seats, the Liberals were a few seats short of a majority. King had won, but the regional and racial biases in the parties' representation in Parliament meant that his task would be a hard one.

King's situation was immediately clear to everyone. In an editorial on the election results, the Toronto-based *Canadian Forum* observed, "The great task of statesmanship which lies before Mr. King is to heal these wounds that have been opened in the body politic. No federation can prosper, or even exist permanently, if they are allowed to fester." True enough. So, too, seemed the *Forum's* last word, "The man who can restore and foster a spirit of unity between city and country, between Ontario and Quebec on the one hand and Ontario and the West on the other hand, is the man of destiny."

Mackenzie King was determined that he would be that man of destiny. Instinctively, he believed that he could heal the breach with the West by bringing the Progressives into his government and taking Crerar and other Progressive leaders into the cabinet. In this way, he could make the Liberal party strong again on the Prairies and in rural Ontario to make it a truly national party; he could also press it toward progressive

Mackenzie King speaking at Brampton, Ontario, during the general election of 1925. Note the two microphones. This was the first general election in which radio played an important part.
Ontario Archives, 3117 #2.

policies, much in line with his own inclinations. "I want, if I can," he wrote his brother, "to have the West feel that I am its friend. . . . I am seeking to bring about . . . a coalescence of Liberal and Progressive forces whereby a new, strong, vigorous, united, solid Liberal Party, representative of the will and the wish of the great body of the people" will be formed.

But King's hope clashed with the expectations of the Prairie and Ontario farmers who distrusted his party as much as the Tories. Crerar was willing to consider joining King's cabinet, but his followers (more those from Ontario than from the West) would not hear of it and King's initial efforts to heal the schism in Liberalism failed. The one chance for a genuinely progressive Liberal party was lost, so King turned, as he had to, to the caucus the electorate had given him. The result was a traditional cabinet, stocked with old men and heavily representative of the eastern financial interests. W. S.

Fielding became the Minister of Finance and Sir Lomer Gouin, Premier of Quebec from 1905 to 1920, the Minister of Justice. George Graham and D. D. McKenzie, along with Fielding the contenders for the Liberal leadership in 1919, also took portfolios. It was better to have them in the cabinet than out of it where they might be powerful foci of discontent.

Discontent with Mackenzie King would come, but only rarely over the next quarter-century and more would it become focused enough to threaten his hold on power. The four years between the elections of 1921 and 1925 were relatively prosperous times for Canada — although employment figures were slow to improve — and the federal government coasted along. The national government's budget generally ran about $350 million each year, of which more than a third was employed to service the national debt, swollen to more than $2.5 billion by the costs of the Great War. The government's revenues were usually in near balance with its expenditures, and Canada received sound, sober administration of its affairs from King's Liberal government.

There was nothing adventurous about the King government. The Prime Minister had failed to bring the Progressives into the cabinet, but he could generally count on their support for "progressive" legislation; and he could always bank on the Progressives' dislike for Meighen's advocacy of high tariffs. Still, King's policy moves were hesitant. His government effectively disbanded the armed forces, leaving only a tiny corporal's guard in a few tattered garrisons across the country. He adjusted railway freight rates to the benefit of the Prairies, and in 1924 he lowered or eliminated the tariff on much machinery used in primary production. These were exceedingly modest alterations, but King ecstatically believed that he had at last produced "an epoch making budget. . . . It will bring us back into power by getting the Progressive forces and ours united. . . . I am happy that I have been true to Liberal tradition, true to the platform of the 1919 convention, true to the pledges I gave the electors in 1921 and true to the people . . ."

In fact, King's budget probably helped the Liberal party's fortunes by speeding the decay of the Progressives. The splits in the Progressive party, that had existed from the first, widened under the pressures of daily confrontations in Parliament. In 1922, Crerar had resigned as leader, frustrated beyond belief by the difficulties of leading a party that was not a party and one that tried to link up group-government theorists with mod-

November, by A. Y. Jackson.
The National Gallery of Canada,
Ottawa.
The serenity of the north was a con-
stant inspiration and a recurring motif
in the paintings of the Group of Seven.

erately advanced liberals. In 1924, the more radical members of the party — soon to be called the Ginger Group — left the Progressive caucus, and the next year seventeen Progressive MPS voted in support of a Liberal government measure despite a caucus decision to oppose it. The Prairie revolt slowly eroded under the influence of relatively good times, the pressures of patronage, and the differences of doctrine.

The Tories, however, showed signs of recovery. Meighen still dominated the House of Commons, delicately stripping skin off the Prime Minister with his rapier phrases in every debate. The excoriating sarcasm, the remorseless logic, and the powerful intellect fell with devastating force on the pomposities and cant of Mackenzie King. "We have heard of government by conviction," Meighen said in one debate in 1922:

we ought really to have government by conviction; but what have we now? We have government by listening. The Prime Minister bereft of opinions himself listens sometimes at an angle of 45 degrees, sometimes at an angle of 90 degrees, listens to the whisper of the corridor, listens for the threats and the growls around, and then all these noises are gathered together, fused into one and the conglomerate emission becomes the tune that he calls the Government policy.

The two men, the Prime Minister and the Leader of the Opposition, grew to despise one another, producing a bitter rivalry in Canadian politics that would not be equalled until the contests between John Diefenbaker and Lester Pearson dominated the pre-Centennial decade.

Meighen's dominance of the Commons was only one aspect of the Tory rebirth. More significant was the election of a Conservative government in Ontario in 1923 under G. Howard Ferguson and the decisive rout of the Progressive party. When this victory was followed in mid-1925 by Conservative successes in provincial elections in New Brunswick and Nova Scotia, the extent of Tory rejuvenation was apparent. The Liberals faced a fight, and when Mackenzie King went to the Governor-General, Viscount Byng, for a dissolution in September, the battle began. Election day would be October 29, 1925.

Like his administration, King's campaign was dull. Reform legislation would have brought him the support of former Progressive voters almost automatically, but there had

Mackenzie King speaking during the election campaign of 1926. In spite of its good intentions, the misspelling of his name in the "Welcome McKenzie King" banner doubtless annoyed him, for he was sensitive on the point. (He would have been vastly displeased if he had known that "Mackenzie" was similarly misspelled in the program for the memorial service held in Westminster Abbey in July 1950!) *Public Archives Canada, C-9064.*

been little of it. Instead, King stressed the need for a majority government and promised to promote immigration. He pledged to eliminate political influence in the operation of the Canadian National Railways and to reform the Senate. Election promises from a party in office always sound hollow; King's were more hollow than most.

The Prime Minister also endorsed a "common sense" tariff, a proposal that drew Meighen's fire. This futile do-nothing government had to be eliminated, he said, and the tariff had to be made sufficiently high to protect Canadian manufacturers from foreign competition. His was the same program that he had fought on in 1921, Meighen admitted, but it was right then and right still: "It was the National Policy as Macdonald had shaped it, and as it has since endured." The Progressives, now led by Robert Forke, also campaigned on their 1921 platform, adding only a promise to construct a railway to Hudson Bay. Standpattism was not only a Liberal trait, and it seemed a reflection of the stability that had been established in the country after the inflation-deflation swings from 1919 to 1922. Perhaps King deserved some credit for that.

If so, the voters were not impressed. When the election came, the Conservatives elected 116 MPs to the Liberals' 99, while the Progressives were reduced to 24 seats and Independents made up the remainder in a Parliament of 245 members. Meighen won only four seats in Quebec: he suffered from a vicious campaign that painted him yet again as the monster who had conscripted Canadian youth in 1917. But in Ontario, the Conservatives swept the boards, winning an incredible 57 per cent of the vote and taking 68 of the 82 seats. In the Prairies, Meighen won 10 seats, King 20, and the Progressives 22, while the Maritimes swung heavily Conservative, giving Meighen 23 seats to King's 6. British Columbia gave the Liberals just three seats while Meighen took 10. It was an impressive Tory resurgence, and a striking commentary on Meighen's ability to recreate the battered Tory party in just four years.

For Mackenzie King, the result was unexpected. He had confidently forecast a small majority for the government, and he was completely unprepared for the losses his party took — and for the loss of his own seat. "Expectations have not been realized," he wrote gloomily in his diary. Yet with that characteristic faith and optimism that sustained him in his crisis-filled hours, he concluded that "all is for the best":

> It looks like a heavy road ahead, but the Progressives may come in with us — a few will be foolish enough not to — then if [Meighen] wins in the House of Commons it looks like another election or great uncertainty again for awhile. . . . The times will continue to improve . . . and we may get thro' a session in which event we will be able to carry on — I have 'faith & courage'. . . .

Although he would waver momentarily, clearly King had no intention of turning the reins of power over to Meighen, at least not until Parliament met and his government lost in a vote of confidence. This was his clear constitutional right, although the Governor General was unhappy about King's choosing to exercise it. In retrospect, the unhappiness of Viscount Byng was important for very shortly his role would be critical.

The Governor General in 1925 was not merely the layer of cornerstones, deliverer of bromides, and recipient of insincere encomiums that he has since become. There was no British High Commissioner in Ottawa to represent the United Kingdom, and the Vice-Regal representative in fact filled a diplomatic role and acted largely as the channel of communication between the Canadian government and his own. In addition, Byng, like his predecessors, had an important constitutional function, for he could refuse his Prime Minister's advice when, for example, he was asked for a dissolution of Parliament and summon the Leader of the Opposition to take over the government of the country. This Byng would do in the summer of 1926. How Mackenzie King reached this momentary nadir of his career and how he used it to defeat Meighen is one of the great political stories in Canadian history.

The voters in 1925 made the Liberal government exceedingly vulnerable to pressures of all kinds. Old-age pensions were squeezed from King's reluctant cabinet early in 1926 by the pressures applied by J. S. Woodsworth and A. A. Heaps, the two Labour MPs, and by King himself. This measure was one that King believed in, but he had hesitated in forcing it on his cabinet. The delicate balance in the House of Commons, however, could justify pressing it — it might be crucial to keep Woodsworth and Heaps happy — and the overall result, King wrote in his diary, was "a really important stroke of work." Less successful for the government was the unfolding scandal in the Department of Customs and Excise.

The Department was in a mess and King knew it. The previous Minister, Jacques Bureau, had been elevated to the Senate before the election and the new Minister, George Boivin, was a willing worker but green. The matter might have become simply another minor tempest in a majority House of Commons, but in the 1926 session it was a government-wrecker. The first intimations of disaster came in February 1926 from a speech by H. H. Stevens, a British Columbia Conservative, a speech that was detailed enough to force the government to create an investigatory special committee. While the committee did its work, the government lowered taxes in its "prosperity budget" and pushed through the old-age pensions bill, supported by the Progressives. The farmers' support would be crucial when the Customs committee produced its report.

The results of the Committee's work were made public on June 16, 1926. Civil servants in the department, it demonstrated, had been involved in liquor smuggling into the United States (where Prohibition was still in force), in the smuggling of automobiles into Canada, and in general and widespread inefficiency and laxity. More serious perhaps, the previous Minister had received gifts of liquor from his Montreal customs collector and a smuggled automobile had been sold to his chauffeur. If only Bureau had been involved, however, the King government might have been able to withstand the Con-

Viscount Byng of Vimy, who as Governor General refused Mr. King's request for a dissolution in 1926 and thereby precipitated the memorable general election held in the following September. This photograph, which somehow suggests a caricature, is from the card sent to King by Lord and Lady Byng for Christmas 1925. It was the last greeting to pass between them.
Public Archives Canada, C-39555.

servative's fire; Boivin was a different matter. And when evidence was presented that Boivin had intervened to delay the execution of a sentence of imprisonment on a convicted smuggler, the Committee's Tory members had their issue. The Committee as a whole refused to vote censure on Boivin, but perhaps the House of Commons would be different. The clean-thinking, clean-living Progressives, if persuaded of the Grits' immorality, could bring down the government.

For Mackenzie King, the next few weeks would be crucial. In Parliament the parties manoeuvred desperately with amendments, subamendments and subsubamendments, all the while courting the Progressives and their swing votes. It would

45

be close either way, and King, studying the estimates of his House strategists, concluded that his course was clear. It would be damaging to the party and the government if it were censured in the House of Commons because of the Customs scandal. Therefore, he would go to the Governor General before the crucial vote and ask for a dissolution. The people of Canada, not simply their representatives in Parliament, could judge the fitness of the government at the polls.

The Prime Minister had the right to seek dissolution. The Governor General had the right to refuse it and he did. King countered with volume after volume of constitutional law, but Byng remained adamant. King would not be given his dissolution and Meighen must get a chance to govern. Faced with this stone wall, Mackenzie King submitted his resignation on Monday, June 28, and announced this sudden turn of events to an unsuspecting and stunned House of Commons that day. There was no longer a Prime Minister, he told Meighen. The next day, Meighen was Prime Minister and the Conservatives were in office.

What had happened? Clearly King had tried desperately to avoid the censure of Parliament on his government, and clearly he had played fast and loose with the traditions and practices of parliamentary government in his efforts to escape. He had demonstrated his ability to govern in a minority House through a long session of Parliament, and he might have been entitled to a dissolution on those grounds alone — but after, not before, the vote on censure. He had been too devious, and he had put Byng, a soldier, after all, into a difficult spot. Taking office virtually without notice, Meighen was rescuing the Governor General. But the Conservative leader was eager, too eager, to obtain power and destroy King once and for all. Meighen's problem arose from the practice of the day that ministers on appointment had to resign their seats and win re-election in a by-election. But how could he name a cabinet in such circumstances unless he adjourned the House of Commons, already near the end of its sessional business, and sent the Members home? His answer, too clever by half, was to name acting ministers from among those members of his caucus who had taken the Privy Councillor's oath previously. This way the session could be concluded, the new government could function, and King could be destroyed once and for all.

Left out of Meighen's calculation was King's extraordinary resilience and tactical cunning. The Tory ministers were acting illegally in carrying on the nation's business until they won by-elections, King reasoned. With an easy if slightly spurious logic, the Grits argued that if the acting ministers were legally administering their departments they ought to have vacated their seats; if they did not hold office legally, then they had no right to govern. This argument did the trick for the Liberals, and Meighen's government was beaten by a single vote cast by a Progressive member who broke a pair, an agreement that he would not vote if the Conservative with whom he was paired also did not vote. Defeated after three days in office, Meighen sought and won the dissolution Byng had denied King.

The new Prime Minister called the election for September 14. To Meighen the issue was simple and compelling: Liberal corruption. Any constitutional issue was completely phony and served only, he said in *Maclean's*, to "provide fuel for those agitators and disloyalists who are constantly plotting national or Imperial arson." Mackenzie King had tried to evade censure "but he was not permitted to do so; he thereupon hatched a constitutional issue to act as a smoke screen. That," the Conservative Prime Minister said, "is the case in a nutshell." Meighen was correct, but other factors were at work. For one, the Conservative party was not united. Meighen had been making gestures to Quebec to win some support there, but every move in that direction provoked a hostile response from zealous party loyalists in Ontario and elsewhere. Worse, Meighen had scant success in winning support from French Canadians regardless of his gestures. Above all the issues was Meighen himself. He was hated as no one in our political history. His great ability made him all the more dangerous, and to many his attitudes to Empire smacked of the most abject colonialism, while his economic nationalism as exemplified by his tariff position split the country.

King was also unloved, but he did not seem so dangerous. He was a devious and tricky man, but his seeming mediocrity made him acceptable by comparison to his opponent. He was a nationalist — did not his stand against the Governor General's actions smack of a rejection of colonialism? He was a moderate on tariff questions, a moderate reformer, a moderate on all things. The constitutional issue, obscuring the corruption in the Liberal administration in the minds of the electorate, came as a heaven-sent opportunity to restore a revived party to office. The *Canadian Forum* observed sardonically that "whatever other results Lord Byng's action may have had, it is certain that in refusing to be guided by Mr. King's advice he saved the bacon of the Liberal party." Exactly. Mr. King's bacon, too.

After the election, the *Forum* noted, "Mr. King's luck is extraordinary." So it was, for the Canadian people returned the Liberals to power with a comfortable majority and 128 seats. Meighen was reduced to 91 seats and the Progressives sank to 20. Again Quebec had destroyed the Conservatives, giving them only 4 seats to King's 60, and not even 53 seats in Ontario could redeem this near shutout. The Prairies too were hard on Meighen: only in Alberta did the Conservatives win a single seat. But the constitutional issue had not by itself swung the election. Issues in fact rarely determine elections, although they tend to dominate the writings of journalists and historians. The subtleties of interpretation involved in assessing Byng's acts and omissions were beyond the public and probably played little part. Probably the election was won for King and his party by the intuitive assessment of the voters that he was safer than Meighen, however brilliant the latter. The election was won by hard slogging in the constituencies and knocking on doors. And the election was won on the loyalty of French Canada to Laurier's memory and its long-lived detestation of Meighen and his conscription bill. Whatever the causes, King was in and Meighen was out. Out of office and out of the leadership of his party the following year.

The experience had been a disillusioning one for Meighen. To be defeated in an election was one thing; to be defeated by Mackenzie King, a man for whom he had only contempt, was another entirely. It was hard to fathom, and about all Meighen could conclude was that the blame was not his but the country's. A flaw in the nation prevented it from being willing to follow the hard, true course. Perhaps Meighen was right.

His successor at the head of Canadian Conservatism was Richard Bedford Bennett, yet another Western lawyer. Born in New Brunswick in 1870, Bennett had moved to Calgary in 1897 where his law career prospered mightily. He dabbled in high finance, aided by his New Brunswick crony, Max Aitken, the future Lord Beaverbrook, and his law practice came to include the Canadian Pacific Railway. By 1926, he also controlled the E. B. Eddy Paper Company and had become a millionaire. His political career had started in the Assembly of the Northwest Territories in 1898, and then after defeats in his attempts to get to Ottawa he was elected in 1911. During the war he was Director General of National Service from 1916

Rt. Hon. W. L. Mackenzie King
Lib. 1921 - 1926; 1926 - 1927

Mackenzie King in 1927.
Ontario Archives, S-2630.

to 1917 in which capacity he organized the first (and abortive) national registration of manpower. For a brief period he served as Meighen's Minister of Justice in 1921 and he held three portfolios in Meighen's abbreviated 1926 government, but he and his nominal leader had never been close. Bennett was a match for Meighen in singlemindedness and the two had been contenders for the leadership of the Tory West under Borden, a contest Meighen won. Now a Conservative convention in 1927 had chosen him to oppose Mackenzie King and to restore the party to power once more.

The new Tory leader was a bachelor, a large portly man who dressed like a millionaire and looked like a captain of industry. His intellectual power was probably less than his predecessor's, but he had intelligence and ability, and he could deliver a good speech in a booming voice. He enjoyed making decisions, and to Bennett politics were no different from industry or finance. A man worked hard and if he produced the goods he was rewarded; if not he was sacked. In his view, King could not produce and hence he should be let go by the shareholders. For Mackenzie King, so recently freed of the curse of Arthur Meighen, Bennett was almost more of the same: "He will be a difficult opponent, apt to be very unpleasant, and give a nasty tone to public affairs."

But at least King did not have to think about an election for a few years. After 1926, there was little excitement in Canadian politics. It was government as usual, with every effort being made to reduce expenditures and to lower the public debt, with a budget praised when it was lower than the previous year's, with taxes always going down. In many ways the late 1920s were halcyon years for Canada. Industry expanded rapidly and the Gross National Product continued to climb, reaching $6.1 billion in 1929. The country's population passed 10 million in that same year, and few could see clouds on the horizon. The twentieth century may not have belonged to Canada, but Canadians enjoyed their life in its third decade.

3

The Roaring Twenties

THE ECONOMIC AND SOCIAL problems that confronted Mackenzie King when he became leader of the Liberal party in
1919 were indeed severe. The national hysteria that had char-
acterized the strained war years was still remembered, while the
frenetic economic growth of the boom years at the beginning
of the century had not yet been completely digested into the
body politic. Labour and capital were at war; the rural population was in flux with mass migrations to the cities occurring in
every province; relations between French and English were
worse than at any time since the execution of Riel in 1885; and
the church was actively crusading for a more humane way of
life for those in dire straits. Canada was a society in the throes
of change in 1919.

Yet after just a few years all these strains seemed temporarily eased. The farmers' protests had been muted and the
Progressives were largely absorbed back into the old parties.
Labour had been defeated in the Winnipeg General Strike;
working-class militants were few and far between. French and
English would never really trust one another, but the Liberal
party effectively combined the two races together in a national
organization, and the Diamond Jubilee anniversary of Confederation in 1927 was a time of celebration in all parts of the
country. Prosperity had been the salve to heal the national
wounds, and even if the benefits of wealth were imperfectly
distributed — and they were — there was enough money,
enough growth for the rifts and divisions to be temporarily
forgotten.

Some of this calm was Mackenzie King's doing. He consciously devoted himself and his party to restoring the placid-
ities of an earlier day, and he was particularly successful in

bringing the West and Quebec back into a national consensus. King made his party into an agency for blurring differences. Key questions were not resolved, but they were shelved so skillfully that they seemed to disappear. Of course, prosperity helped, but like every politician Mackenzie King was convinced that good times were directly attributable to his wise stewardship of affairs. It was a good time to be alive, and everything was for the best in the best of all possible worlds.

In a sense, the 1920s were the first modern decade as we would understand it today. Airplanes were a frequent sight in the sky, the movies were everywhere and entertainment was cheap, radio was becoming increasingly popular, and the era of the automobile had begun. The society was recognizably similar to our own.

For the most part, the automobile was the decisive factor in this transition to modernism. The car changed the life of the people in the cities and on the farms, while the development of the truck altered industry by improving shipping. In 1918, there were just over a quarter of a million motor vehicles in Canada; at the end of the 1920s, there were four times as many, and the impact of the ready availability of personal, cheap transportation was enormous.

Even in 1924 Bay Street in Toronto had its traffic tie-ups, though the congestion was no doubt aggravated by motorists who had ignored the "No Parking" signs under the street lamps.
Public Archives Canada, PA-54398 (on loan from the Toronto Transit Commission).

"The greatest improvement in transportation facilities since the invention of the steam locomotive," one Progressive Member of Parliament called the auto in 1926, and he was right. For the rural dweller, this was particularly true, for the car reduced isolation, much as had the telephone. If isolation could be ended, farming would be more attractive as a profession, and the ceaseless exodus of sons and daughters to the bright lights of Regina, Edmonton, or Toronto might be checked. But the cost of even a small roadster was high in the 1920s, close to $1000, and that price was simply out of the reach of the average worker whose total yearly earnings ranged between $800 and $1300, with most clustered at the lower end. The automobile was a rich man's toy in the cities, but on the farms it was a vital necessity.

The automobile increased the demand for better roads, which had been necessary for years in any case. But while a horse and buggy or wagon could make do with muddy tracks, the automobile could not. In 1925 in all of Canada there were only 47,000 miles of surfaced road, a category that included gravel roads. Only 6100 miles of non-urban roads were paved. At the end of the decade, after much agitation and enormous outlays of public money, there were only 80,000 miles of surfaced roads and still more than 150,000 miles of improved earth roads. Nonetheless, the business executive who would drive from Toronto to Montreal in an expensive Rolls-Royce was already a regular sight, and one Member of Parliament bemoaned the threat to the railways posed by road transport:

> The automobiles and motor trucks are securing nearly all of the local traffic by which the railways have so far been sustained, and where that competition is going to end I am at a loss to know. . . . Toronto business houses are able to have their telephone orders given to outlying towns filled in the space of a few hours . . . the motor truck will be at the customer's door that afternoon.

The decline of the railway was at hand.

Visionaries could see this decline in the mid-1920s, but they were few and far between. The 1920s seemed to be a great railway decade, and the capital invested in the tracked networks almost doubled from $2 billion in 1919 to $3.9 billion in 1929, although total mileage rose only from 50,691 in 1919 to 55,813 in 1929. More significant was the diversification that marked the efforts of Canadian Pacific Railway and Canadian National Railways. The CPR held huge tracts of land all

Parliament Hill on July 1, 1927, when Canada celebrated the 60th anniversary of Confederation. Little notice could be taken of the 50th anniversary in 1917, as World War I was raging. *Public Archives Canada, C-18068.*

across the country and controlled mines and natural resources worth millions. Under aggressive management it expanded its operations to include steamships, hotels, and resorts. In 1929, for example, the CPR opened the Royal York Hotel in Toronto, soon to be one of the largest hotels in the world. The CNR, a publicly owned system formed out of bankrupt and near-bankrupt private systems during and after the Great War, competed for passengers, freight, and hotel guests with the privately owned CPR; its President and Chairman, like that of its great competitor, was a public figure of note whose personal activities merited three or four pages each year in the *Canadian Annual Review*, the record of each year's activities.

Air travel, by contrast, was still virtually unknown. Only in the bush, in areas where road and rail travel was unavailable, was the small two- or three-place aircraft a common

The six largest of the 53 bells comprising the carillon in the Peace Tower of the Parliament Buildings arriving in Ottawa by train. The heaviest of the six weighed over 11 tons. The carillon was dedicated by the Governor General on July 1, 1927, as part of the celebrations marking the diamond jubilee of Confederation. *Public Archives Canada, C-19219.*

The year 1936 marked the 50th anniversary of the inauguration of Canadian Pacific's transcontinental passenger service. On June 28, in celebration of the event, this specially decorated train left Windsor Street Station in Montreal for the Pacific Coast. *Canadian Pacific.*

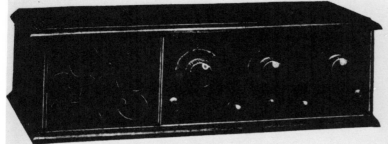

5-Tube Freshman Masterpiece Set, with Loud Speaker Built In, Complete $133.50

A—A set which combines beauty with efficiency. The cabinet is of selected wood in mahogany finish, with built-in loud speaker. All terminals for batteries, etc., are at the back. Equipment is as follows:

80 amp. hour Hart storage battery.
2 Burgess batteries, No. 2306.
Set of phones and plug.
5 Radiotron U.V. 201A tubes.
Complete aerial outfit.

This 5-tube Masterpiece Set, $133.50

Freshman Set, Without Loud Speaker, $118.50

B—With an attractive mahogany case comes this set, which will give the clear tone and long range characteristic of all Freshman Masterpiece Sets.
Complete equipment includes:
80 amp. hour Hart storage battery.
5 Radiotron U.V. 201A tubes.
2 Burgess batteries, No. 2306.
One set of phones and plug.
One complete aerial outfit.

Complete set, without loud speaker, $118.50.

B
$118.50

The "Laundry Maid"

13-109 The principle of this strong, well-made **Washing Machine** of seasoned wood is the open type. The barred rubbing board, working on a corrugated surface, squeezes and rubs the clothes at the same time. It is easily adjusted to different-sized washings. There are no intricate parts or castings to get out of order and it should give years of service. Measures 32 x 21 ins. at top, and is 24½ ins. high. Note the low cost to you.
Price............ **10.25**

OPPOSITE The cover of an Eaton's mail-order catalogue of the 1920s. It cleverly advertised both the fashions of the day and the fact that every post office was in effect a branch office of Eaton's.
Archives, Eaton's of Canada Limited.

The loudspeaker, which liberated listeners from wires and earphones, introduced radio as we know it today. This advertisement from a 1925 issue of *Eaton's News Weekly* illustrates early cabinet models.
Archives, Eaton's of Canada Limited.

In the 1920s, much household equipment was still primitive by present-day standards. This hand washing machine was a popular item in Eaton's 1926 Spring and Summer Catalogue. Electric washers were becoming available, but many people could not afford them and in most rural areas electricity was not yet available.
Archives, Eaton's of Canada Limited.

A MAN'S SUMMER CLOTHES!

GOLF KNICKERS

A—Good-looking golf knickers and plus fours have arrived with the golf season. They come in novelty tweeds of smooth or rough finish, with a wide variety of small patterns, in greys and fawns. Those sketched in diamond check are of two tones of grey, made with the new combination buckle and button fastening at the knee. Sizes 30 to 42, $6.00. Others in smooth grey or fawn novelty tweeds, $5.00.

CREAM FLANNELS

B—With days of tennis and sailing near, and evenings of Summer dances approaching, cream flannel trousers become important in a man's wardrobe. Well cut trousers of heavy cream flannel, finished with cuffs, in sizes 30 to 40, are $10.00.

C $35.00

A $6.00

B $10.00

D $35.00

E $25.00

TROPICAL TWEEDS

C—Finely woven tropical tweeds are extremely good-looking for men's wear. Three-piece suits are made up in greys, showing vague striped patterns, or in navy with a white and yellow hair line. They come in men's and young men's single and double-breasted models. Sizes 34 to 46, $35.00.

FLANNEL SUITS

D—Flannel is to be used extensively this season to make smart Summer suits for men and young men. Patterns include novelty diamond checks in light or dark lovat, plain light and dark greys, blue, grey and sand. They are in three-piece styles, single or double-breasted, half lined with artificial silk. Sizes 34 to 46, $35.00.

MOHAIR SUITINGS

E—Suits of lustre or mohair are perhaps the coolest, most comfortable thing for business men's Summer wear. New models are now here, showing black mohair with white hair lines. There is a choice of several styles in models for tall, short and stout men. Sizes 35 to 48, $25.00.

Men's Clothing, Second Floor, James Street

The average man's suits varied relatively little in styling and price during the decade. This advertisement appeared in the spring of 1926.
Archives, Eaton's of Canada Limited.

Some of Eaton's fashion offerings for the 1920 spring and summer season. Note the prices. Other dresses were priced as low as $3.50.
Archives, Eaton's of Canada Limited.

59

The automobile at its pre-Depression peak: the auto show at the Canadian National Exhibition in Toronto in 1929, a few weeks before the stock market crash. Many well-known makes would disappear during the Depression or survive only briefly. *Public Archives Canada, PA-52954.*

sight, and its users were the geologists, the miners, the surveyors, and the foresters. The bush pilots, almost all veterans of the Royal Flying Corps of the Great War, were opening up the North and becoming the explorers of the twentieth century. Their small planes carried substantial quantities of freight, and they made mining possible in some areas for the first time. By 1921, 29 companies were operating aircraft. Regular air-mail service between Victoria and Vancouver had been in operation since the year before. The first regular air service carrying passengers began in 1922, linking Haileybury in Ontario to Rouyn in northern Quebec; in 1927 a regular passenger service between some larger cities was started. But Canada had no national system of air routes, and would not have one until Trans-Canada Air Lines was established by the federal government in 1937. Air travel was ahead of its time in the 1920s, although the barnstorming pilot doing Immelmann rolls was a common sight at country fairs and urban exhibitions.

The improvement in individual transportation probably had most impact on the national consciousness in the cities. The car made the countryside close and convenient; it also gave the children of the middle and upper classes a place away from parental scrutiny, something that had not always been readily available before. The automobile revolutionized the moral standards of a generation, lending an easy if spurious freedom to those who could acquire the status symbol of a car. Roadhouses sprang up across the country to provide music, entertainment, and alcohol for those able to reach them and pay the price; Canadians tried to emulate the giddy flapper atmosphere of the Prohibition-ridden United States. Movies and radio brought the latest fads to Canada as soon as they were established in the United States. The barriers of distance and time that had preserved Canada from Americanization in the past fell like tenpins.

The ready availability of liquor and beer in almost all parts of Canada eased this shift in public morality. Prohibition had been enforced in Canada during the war when booze was readily portrayed as a servant of the devil that hindered the war effort. Huge majorities in plebiscites voted for prohibition in the Prairie provinces, and the Union government at the end

A Fokker Universal mono-plane, a popular work-horse in the early days of flying in the North. It had three special attractions: an air-cooled radial engine that would not freeze, an enclosed heated cabin that added greatly to the comfort of the crew, and adaptability. It could be quickly equipped with wheels, floats, or skis, as conditions might require. *Manitoba Archives.*

of 1917 imposed its own prohibition on any beverage containing more than 2.5 per cent alcohol. Canadian prohibition lapsed in 1919, although the various provinces continued it in force for varying lengths of time. But prohibition, it was soon clear, seemed almost as bad a social evil as the drunkenness it sought to eliminate. Bootleggers proliferated, serving the local markets and expanding their operations to serve the thirsty United States. The potential for profit seemed great enough to justify the risks. In Bienfait, Saskatchewan, the town "boozorium" sold a case of 12 bottles for $50, but in the United States that case could bring $300. Under Saskatchewan law, it was illegal to sell whiskey for consumption in the province, but not at all illegal to export it to the United States, even if its consumption was forbidden under American law. The inevitable result of this kind of chaos was the entry of mobsters onto the scene, with murder and armed robbery added to the usual risks involved in smuggling across an international border. Of course, bootleg liquor was sold in Canada too, and all too often a bad batch blinded unlucky drinkers.

Gradually, many of the prohibitionists came to believe that they had been wrong in advocating an end to drink. The world "is turned upside down by bottleggers, bandits and bank-robbers," a Manitoba crusader against prohibition said in 1923. "The cure is ten times worse than the disease." So it seemed to the majority in most of the provinces, and the decade saw prohibition virtually ended. In its place throughout most of the country stood government-run liquor stores and severe and capricious government regulations determining how and where people could drink. Liquor was available to those of age, providing they segregated themselves by sex. That great Canadian institution, the men's and women's beverage rooms, had been created. But now it was legal once again for any red-blooded Canadian to drink him- or herself silly — and the provincial revenues would be the beneficiary.

The return of legal drinking was a defeat for morality — "It is a lovers of pleasure more than a lovers of God age," a member of the Women's Christian Temperance Union wrote in 1924 — and a setback to those who struggled to reform the social order. Prohibition had been motivated by a desire to do "good works," but it was so all-embracing in its unsophistication that it did great harm to the society it tried to reform. Less unsuccessful were other efforts of the church in Canada, as the social gospel — a creed directed at improving the lot of the people and meeting the social needs of men — burgeoned

Temperance supporters made a valiant effort to have prohibition continue as the law of the land after the end of World War I. This appeal to the people appeared in newspapers from coast to coast in 1919. Ironically, it was published just as the Volstead Act, with all its unforseen consequences, made nationwide prohibition law in the United States. In spite of the efforts of the Dominion Prohibition Committee and other organizations, seven of the nine provinces repealed prohibition between 1921 and 1927.

Metropolitan Toronto Library Board.

Temperance Platform

The Dominion Prohibition Committee are asking:

1. That the Prime Minister and Government of Canada be requested to take the steps necessary to continue in effect the provisions of the Order-in-Council of March 11th, 1918, (P.C. 589) by having the same embodied in Legislation to be enacted by the Parliament of Canada.

2. That the legislation so enacted be continued in effect until such time as a vote of the electors of the Dominion of Canada shall have been taken on the question of its continuance or dis-continuance.

3. That the vote on this question be taken at a date to be fixed by the Government of Canada at least six months prior to the day of voting and with due respect to the restoration to civil life in Canada of the Canadian soldiers now overseas.

Who Want Prohibition ?

Ask—

1. The Business men and Industrial leaders whom you know.
2. The working men and working women whom you know.
3. The Mothers, Wives and Children whom you know.
4. The Soldier Citizens of Canada whom you know.
5. The farmers whom you know.

We know that

1. Every Church and Religious Denomination in Canada has pronounced in favor of Prohibition through its Executive Boards and Church Leaders.
2. Practically all School-teachers, Doctors, Public Health Officers, City Relief Officers and Social Workers in Canada are in favor of Prohibition.
3. The Provincial Governments, the Courts and the Police have learned that Prohibition reduces crime and disorder and promotes Peace and Prosperity.

Prohibition in Canada

An Open Letter to the People of Canada

𝔗HIS STATEMENT is being published in the Daily Papers in every Province of Canada in order to call attention to the following facts:

First fact: Every Province in Canada now has a Temperance Law in force with the exception of Quebec. On May first, 1919, the Quebec Temperance Law will come into force.

Second fact: The Dominion Government passed Legislation under the powers granted in "The War Measures Act," which prohibited for the period of the war and twelve months thereafter, Importation, Manufacture and Interprovincial Shipment of liquor for drinking purposes. This Legislation is necessary to make effective that of the Provinces.

Third fact: The people of Canada want this Legislation continued in effect until the Citizens of Canada, including all the soldiers, shall have had an opportunity to vote on the question of making it permanent.

Fourth fact: There is an insidious and far-reaching propaganda now being carried on which aims to discredit the Prohibitory Laws and restore liquor-drinking for the personal profit of the Liquor-Seller.

Fifth fact: The requisite number of State Legislatures in the United States having adopted the Prohibition Amendment, Canada must act in harmony with it or become the dumping ground for liquor and its unfortunate victims.

and spread throughout the country. One indication of this new Christianity was the labour churches that had their heyday between 1919 and 1921: a small but influential group of clerics tried hard to bring religion to the working people. Jesus had died for justice and brotherhood, these clerics believed, and justice and brotherhood similarly were the goals of the labour movement. The community of interest seemed close, and the pressure of the labour church advocates helped push the established orthodoxies into a more concerned position. As a result, the churches found themselves concerned with working conditions, housing, welfare, and a wide range of community problems. Some could see in this turning toward the world a spiritual bankruptcy; others thought that religion at last had acquired a relevance to the great mass of the people.

If part of the church was interested in breaking down barriers, another part was desperately concerned with maintaining and strengthening them. Bigotry of a kind that people only whisper about today was a very real part of everyday life. Such terms of abuse as drunken Indian, wop, sheeny, frog, kike, hunky were common usage and employed even by the better educated. For a long time only the Indians had been present to be scorned, shunted off to reservations, and destroyed by the overwhelming force of white civilization. But by 1921, some 1.5 million Canadians were of neither Anglo-Saxon nor French stock and these people, many of whom had chosen Canada consciously as their residence and who had worked long and hard to carve out a life for themselves, were treated with prejudice and hate. One overt expression of this bigotry was the Ku Klux Klan, an organization that brought many ministers and God-fearing Christians together in the 1920s, particularly in Saskatchewan, in response to fears that immigration would produce an eventual Catholic majority in the province and in the country.

Originally American, the Klan came to Alberta and Saskatchewan in the carpetbags of two entrepreneurs in 1926. The Klan's creed was all-embracing:

> The Klan believes in Protestantism, racial purity, Gentile economic freedom, just laws and liberty, separatism of church and state, pure patriotism, restrictive and selective immigration, freedom of speech and press, law and order, higher moral standards.

In Prairie terms, that creed was transformed easily into an attack on "the slag and the scum, the men who eat spaghetti

OPPOSITE Canadian Pacific travel poster advertising steamship service to major European centres. *Metropolitan Toronto Library Board.*

A Ku Klux Klan gathering in Kingston in 1927. *Public Archives Canada, PA-87848.*

and hot dog and rye bread for lunch or suck on a limburger cheese, the men who came to Canada with tags on them telling their destination." Clearly, then, the Klan's attack in the West was directed against the great wave of immigrants from southern and central Europe that was pouring into Canada. The West's British nationality was jeopardized by this torrent of foreigners, and the Klan found ready converts. Its ultra-Protestantism, keyed to appeal to fundamentalist Christians, gave it support from many Baptist and United Church pulpits. Many newspapers also offered the Klan sympathetic coverage, and there was a potential for serious trouble in the Klan's steady growth. Fortunately, in Saskatchewan Premier J. G. Gardiner lashed out at the bigotry of the movement and its supporters, and many sensible clergymen joined in. The fate of the movement seemed temporarily sealed in 1927 when two leaders absconded with the Klan funds, an estimated $100,000, but the Klan was still strong enough in 1929 to help support the Conservative party under Dr. Anderson in a successful election in Saskatchewan.

Hateful as it was, the Klan expressed a popular fear of "these dirty, ignorant garlic-smelling, non-preferred continentals." Immigration of the "wrong" sort frightened the

English-speaking Canadian and those who considered the Roman Catholic church to be still the whore of Rome. (It also worried French Canadians who feared that the newcomers would be assimilated eventually into the majority, leaving them even more tightly locked into a minority position in the country.) Almost 1,250,000 newcomers came to Canada during the decade of the 1920s, and hundreds of thousands settled in the West. To some, it was necessary to fill the Prairies with settlers, producers, and consumers, and settlement of any kind by any race, creed, or colour was a good thing. But to others, perhaps to a majority, immigration that upset the cultural balance was a danger. The war years had seen the growth of hostility to "foreigners," and the Winnipeg General Strike of 1919, popularly believed to have been the work of "aliens," had exacerbated the trend. Other factors, such as the arrival of the "peculiar" Hutterites in 1918 in Alberta, helped increase prejudice. The depression and deflation of 1921 made the competition for jobs more serious and increased concern about those immigrants who were willing to work for less than "white man's wages." One of the leading Prairie spokesmen against the "mongrelization" of Canada was G. E. Lloyd of Saskatchewan: "The essential question before Canadians today is this: Shall Canada develop as a British nation within the empire, or will she drift apart by the introduction of so much alien blood that her British instincts will be paralyzed?" A man like Lloyd, while more respectable to polite society than the Klansmen with their white hoods and burning crosses, preached the same racist doctrine.

The attitudes of the day were based on the popular conception of what "science" had to say about race, anthropology and psychology. The races could mix, but the result might be a weaker mongrel, not a superior specimen. One writer, no bigot, wrote, "If we mean by assimilation a process that moulds racial stocks into something else we are flying in the face of what every stockbreeder knows. . . . No melting pot can make a Slav, an Italian, or Frenchman, an Anglo-Saxon. Racial qualities, vices and instincts will remain. They may, however, be modified by environment, sublimated into some other form." Perhaps. But this could not still the fears of men like Stephen Leacock, Canada's great humorist whose writings on serious topics were full of the cliches and prejudices of the age:

Still more important is the economic and racial character of the immigrants. . . . They no longer consist of the strenuous, the adventurous, the enterprising; they are not, except in a minor degree, political exiles or religious refugees; they are animated by no desire to build up a commonwealth of freedom to replace an ungrateful fatherland. They are, in great measure, mere herds of the proletariat of Europe, the lowest classes of industrial society, without home and work, fit objects indeed for philanthropic pity, but indifferent material from which to build the commonwealth of the future. They encounter no difficulty in their passage, or none that is comparable to the stern process of earlier history, when the cruel "evolution" of Nature winnowed out the strong from the weak and the resolute from the feeble. (Stephen Leacock, "Canada and the Immigration Problem," *National and English Review*, April 1911.)

Against this view, all that could be put up was that famous phrase uttered in 1922 by Sir Clifford Sifton, longtime Minister of the Interior in the Laurier government and the man who had settled the West: "I think a stalwart peasant in a sheepskin coat, born on the soil, whose forefathers had been farmers for generations, with a stout wife and half-a-dozen children, is good quality."

The irony of the situation, and sad irony it is, was that even immigrants from the British Isles ran into prejudice. "No Englishman need apply" was a phrase that governed hiring in parts of the West. The upper-class English were despised for their "snooty" ways, while the lower class were considered to be so ground down by circumstance at home that they could not make good Canadians. Irish Catholics were particularly condemned.

Some of the attitudes toward the English were a sign of the development of distinctive Canadian traits. Canadians were British, yes, but different in their Britishness even from the people who had formed the pattern. The war had put thousands and thousands of men from all across Canada together and into contact with their forebears. Perhaps to their surprise, soldiers discovered that a private from Manitoba and one from Nova Scotia had more in common than either did with a Lancashire corporal or a London gunner. This contact, combined with a distaste for the way individual Britons looked down on Canadians as "colonials," helped produce a resentment on the one hand and an awareness of distinctiveness on the other. The isolationism induced by the casualties of the war helped foster this combined attitude, as did the efforts by Canadian political leaders like Mackenzie King to enhance

Dr. C. H. Best (left) and Dr. F. G. Banting, of Toronto, photographed in 1921, a few months before their research on diabetes resulted in a major advance in medicine — the discovery of insulin. The dog was one of the de-pancreatized animals used in their experiments. *Academy of Medicine, Toronto, Picture Collection 71.5.74.*

Canadian status in the world.

However real this nationalism, it did not stop Canadians — and particularly the native born — from looking for greener pastures. By the thousands Canadians deserted the harsh climate of Canada, the seasonal nature of employment, the racism, and stratified social structure for the United States. In 1920, 90,000 left, 72,000 the next year, 46,000 the year after, and fully 117,000 in 1923. Life was easier and better in the United States, it offered more opportunity, higher pay, a freer way of life. The best-educated, the most ambitious, the ones Canada could least afford to lose, left. The brain drain cost the country an incalculable amount.

The sterility of life in Canada also drove out artists, writers, actors, and scholars. Canada was not and had never been a country where people who worked with their heads, where people who tried to create ideas, paintings, or sculpture, had thrived. The tenor of the nation was too pragmatic for that, too much work had to be done for time to be wasted on such things. The result for the most part had been a dearth of Canadian literature, paintings, or sculpture, but in the 1920s the new nationalism that had begun to grip Canadians had its artistic counterparts.

The Group of Seven were the foremost proponents of nationalism in Canadian art. They focused on the land, the trees, the lakes, and the rocks of Canada, and they presented a living landscape, a recognizable picture of the world around them to Canadians. This style was a far cry from the previous generation of painters who had tried to graft a European style onto Canadian painting, and the Group of Seven met with criticism. Some angry critics scorned the Group as the "Hot Mush School"; others complained that the landscapes the Group portrayed did not at all resemble the countryside around them. But nationalism was in the Seven's work, and the nationalism they helped to foster gave them a status — and an eventual market.

Of course, the cultural standards of the day were low. In 1927, for example, the Canadian National Exhibition in Toronto provided the scene for a scandal when two or three nudes were exhibited in the art display. The pictures were condemned as indecent, immoral, and an affront to decent womanhood. Crowds of giggling schoolboys surrounded the exhibit, the sensationalist Toronto press charged, but one later writer observed that he merely found numbers of the middle-aged displaying "unusual interest" at short range while at a distance the younger generation were "casting at them sidelong glances of shamefaced curiosity." Silliness and small-town culture prevailed even in the larger cities.

Literature had no Group of Seven to capture the lives of the people. The great Canadian novel was not written in the 1920s, and the popular writers of the day, like Ralph Connor, are scarcely remembered today. Connor's many books were largely sentimental melodrama, but very revealing in portraying the stereotypes of race and belief that motivated Canadians of the middle class. However, a genuine Canadian school of poets was in the making: perhaps the first sign was the publication of E. J. Pratt's *Newfoundland Verse* in 1923. In short lines, as in "The Shark," Pratt demonstrated a power of verse that had hitherto been lacking:

Then out of the harbour,
With that three-cornered fin
Shearing without a bubble the water,
Lithely,
Leisurely,
He swam, —
That strange fish
Tubular, tapered, smoke-blue,
Part vulture, part wolf,
Part neither — for his blood was cold.

Other poets like A. J. M. Smith, Leo Kennedy, and Dorothy Livesay had already begun their equally fruitful careers. But, as a critic wrote with some discouragement in the *Canadian Forum* (that Toronto monthly was itself a sign of the times), "The trouble is that, born to hew wood and draw water, we are trying desperately to be literary, to have a real renaissance." This situation posed problems because "Canada is probably the most backward country for its population in the civilized world, and the quickest way to get rid of this unpleasant family skeleton is to abolish critical standards and be a booster. We don't know what to write, but by jingo if we do have the pen, we have the ink, we have the paper, too." The result had been bulky anthologies of trash — "an honest and sincere desire to establish a completely parochial scale of values." Cultural nationalism then could be a danger to the development of a sound literature.

Academics generally, and Canadian historians more specifically, avoided cultural nationalism. Frank Underhill, the brilliant essayist and scholar who taught at the University of Toronto, wrote in 1929 that historians in Canada suffered

WHAT'S IN THE AIR TO-NIGHT?

Archives, Eaton's of Canada Limited.

Radio broadcasting in Canada began in 1919. In 1923 the CNR formed a Radio Department that built up a national network from which the present CBC networks have been developed. At first, studios were simple affairs: this photograph was taken while Madge Macbeth's play *Superwoman* was being broadcast from station CNRO, Ottawa. Mrs. Macbeth is at the microphone.
Public Archives Canada, C-29468.

"from a belated colonialism. One of the curious features of our present-day Universities, upon which our grandchildren will reflect with wonder, is the fact that the history taught in them is predominantly the history of England and Europe, and that the students are encouraged directly or indirectly to despise the history of their own country and of the continent of which it forms a part." To Underhill, Canadians had to turn to the study of Canada and, he added, the best source of parallels on which they could draw was in the history of the great republic to the south. Underhill was undoubtedly correct. The endless reiterations of Kings and Queens had dulled generations of students, and the Canadian history taught, such as it was, became a ceaseless reiteration of statute after statute, constitution after constitution. To the south, great theses were being argued, great movements considered.

But the influence of the United States on Canada was already very great indeed. In 1914, before the Great War, the United States trailed Britain as an investor in Canada, con-

trolling only 23 per cent of foreign capital. By 1922, U.S. capital had reached 50 per cent of the total foreign investment in the country and by the end of the 1920s it was at 60 per cent, a total of more than $4 billion. To one of the great bankers of Montreal, this was a good thing: "I . . . welcome the flow of money which must assist in the development of our natural resources, give employment to labour, and increase our exports to other countries." Not so, argued those concerned about the future. The statistics were not entirely certain, but it seemed likely that the United States already controlled half the manufacturing in the country. What would the British say if it were discovered that half their industrial organization was controlled abroad? And how paradoxical that patriots who would fight to the death to prevent one foot of Canadian soil from being occupied by the invader saw no objection to the disposal of Canada's wealth to the highest bidder. The arguments of the 1920s sound distressingly familiar to those of the 1970s; all that has changed is that the percentages of Can-

Originally, radio studio equipment was simple and often improvised. This 1931 photograph shows the crew that produced the sound effects for the *Romance of Canada* series — the first series of historical dramas heard over the air in this country. *Public Archives Canada,* *PA-92386.*

Women in the Toronto of the '20s dressed in the fashion of the times. *James Collection, City of Toronto Archives.*

ada's resources controlled in the United States have increased.

The American presence also threatened in radio broadcasting, one of the true growth industries of the decade. In 1920 the first station in Canada began regular broadcasts in Montreal, just a month after the first U.S. station went into operation. By March 1923, 34 Canadian and 556 American stations had gone on the air, all competing for wavelengths in an essentially unregulated situation. With so many American stations operating close to the Canadian border, however, and with the American stations grouping rapidly into networks that sold time to commercial concerns, the whole course of Canadian radio development came under public scrutiny. Would Canadian listeners tune in to U.S. stations and disregard their own? What effect would this preference for American programming have? An initial response came from an unlikely source — the Canadian National Railways. Under the energetic lead of its president, Sir Henry Thornton, the CNR began organizing a radio network in 1923 and soon its programs (and advertisements for the government-owned railway line) were being carried over stations in Ottawa, Montreal, Toronto, Winnipeg, Saskatoon, Regina, Edmonton, Calgary, Moncton, and Vancouver. By 1929, the CNR network broadcast three hours of programming each day all across the land, and its programs included symphonies, opera, and even historical presentations about "The Romance of Canada." The radio also served to unify the great sprawling country, and the Diamond Jubilee celebrations of 1927 on Parliament Hill, for example, were broadcast across Canada. Of more direct political interest, the radio put politicians into the homes of the voters in a way that had never before been possible: once and for all the new medium ended the political legerdemain that had permitted leaders to promise policy "A" to the Maritimes and a contradictory policy "B" to the West. Consistency had always been a virtue; now radio made it a necessity as well.

What was the proper role of government in controlling broadcasting? This difficult question was put to a Royal Commission in 1928. The next year the Commission provided its answer: Canadian radio listeners wanted Canadian radio broadcasting and to achieve this goal "some form of public ownership, operation and control behind which is the national power and prestige of the whole public of the Dominion of Canada" was necessary. There would be many slips along the way, but that Royal Commission report was the beginning of the process that led to the Canadian Broadcasting Corporation paid for out of public moneys.

Yonge Street, Toronto, on Christmas Eve 1924. Parking was just beginning to be a serious problem. *Public Archives Canada, PA-54394 (from a Toronto Transit Commission photograph loaned to Public Archives Canada).*

The choice for radio had been "the state or the States," as R. B. Bennett noted, and the Canadian government eventually moved to fill the breach. Motion pictures had no such development, with the result that American films totally dominated the Canadian market. The actors and actresses best known to Canadians were those best known to Americans, like Charlie Chaplin, Douglas Fairbanks, Mary Pickford (there was some consolation in that she was Canadian-born) and the Gish sisters. Close to a thousand movie theatres were scattered across Canada by the end of the 1920s, just at the time that talking pictures were becoming available.

In sports, too, American influence was tremendous. Babe Ruth was a Canadian hero, as was Jack Dempsey. But hockey was a Canadian game and although the National Hockey League had a substantial number of American teams by 1925, the players were all Canadian. The great names, the Conachers, Howie Morenz, Lester Patrick, and others were household words.

The American influence was probably strongest where it was least noticeable — in everyday life. The brand-name products that Canadians bought, the clothes they wore, the expressions they used, and the fads they eagerly snapped up were all American. The two North American nations had been pushed together by geography and politics, and gradually they became remarkably similar. Of course, Canada was less rich and the climate imposed constraints, but otherwise the trend was toward a similar destiny. If spiritualism became the "in" thing in New York could Toronto or Montreal be far behind? Table-rapping seances, tea-cup readings, and tarot cards quickly became a staple of middle-class life. If Dr. Coué and his banal philosophy that everything was for the best became popular in Los Angeles could Vancouver avoid it? Not at all — soon hundreds walked the streets mumbling to themselves, "Every day in every way I am getting better and better." Radio and movies accelerated this trend, as did the free interchange across the borders. These developments were beneficial to Canadians in many ways, for the United States was an advanced society setting the pace for the rest of the world in a host of areas. Unfortunately, the easy flow of ideas destroyed any prospect for the development of a distinctive Canadian society. After the 1920s the best Canadians could aspire to was to be part of a North American cultural region.

4
The Bust

THE BOOM OF THE 1920s had seen Canada grow and prosper. The benefits had not been equally distributed – they never are – but enough wealth had trickled downward so that all classes of the society were probably as well off as they had ever been, with one exception. Farmers in all parts of the country had watched their real incomes drop throughout the last part of the decade, a decline especially serious in the West. Wheat prices in particular had declined, down more than 25¢ a bushel for No. 1 Northern wheat between 1925 and 1928. But agricultural prices always fluctuated, people said, and there could be no doubt that Canada was moving forward. The Gross National Product had exceeded $6 billion for the first time in 1928; there was money in the country and money to be made.

Speculators got rich throughout the last years of good times. People trafficked in land, in mining stocks, in commodity futures. All too often virtually no cash was put up for these purchases, whole transactions being floated on very small margin. This system worked adequately when the market kept rising, but if a collapse came, all those with millions in paper profits and offers to buy stock at certain prices at certain dates would suddenly find themselves broken and bankrupted.

The piper was paid at the end of October 1929. On October 24, the stock market on Wall Street suffered a drastic fall in values, and the same day the Winnipeg Grain Exchange was battered by a drop in prices. A few days later the wave of selling at panic prices spread to the Montreal and Toronto stock exchanges. Early in November, the European markets rallied, but on November 13 the bottom dropped out again. Even the best blue chip stocks lost 30, 40, or 50 per cent and more of their inflated pre-crash values, while less solid offerings were wiped out completely.

The signs of a crash had existed for some time. Rising interest rates had begun to slow down business expansion, and there were signs of decreasing employment in key sectors of the economy. The wheat market was low too, thanks to a drought in June that cut yield, and suddenly people began to realize once again that prosperity in Canada was inextricably linked with agriculture. If wheat sales dropped drastically, for example, rail freight movement decreased; since the railways were the largest employers and greatest financial concerns in the nation, every aspect of life was soon affected.

Every aspect except the Prime Minister and his government. To Mackenzie King, the downturn was simply a temporary adjustment of no great concern. Probably it was even desirable that the worst speculators should get their fingers burned. Much more important to King was the general election that he would have to call fairly soon, and he worried more about the effect that increasing American tariffs might have on his prospects than he did about the stock market's down-

R. B. Bennett.
Public Archives Canada,
C-7731.

turn. King was blind, but so was everyone. No one had conceived of an end to prosperity; no one had thought that world trade would collapse; no one had realized that Canada, as an exporter of primary products, would be hurt as much or more than any country in the world by the crash. No one; not Mackenzie King, not R. B. Bennett had foreseen the disaster.

The timing of the election was crucial for success and King canvassed all the factors. Economic conditions were not good, he realized early in 1930, but they might get worse. The government's budget, introduced in Parliament on May 1, reported a surplus of government revenues and promised yet another reduction in taxes. The tariff on British goods was lowered, an appeal to the British-born, while the tariff on American products was raised, a clever attempt to undercut the Conservative leader's demands for increased duties to encourage Canadian production. It was a good budget from the Liberal viewpoint. "Switch trade from U.S. to Britain," King wrote, "that will be the cry & it will sweep the country I believe. We will take the flag once more out of the Tory hands."

As the Depression deepened, finding sleeping quarters became more and more of a problem for the unemployed. In this room four men shared the bed while three others slept on the floor.
Public Archives Canada, C-13236.

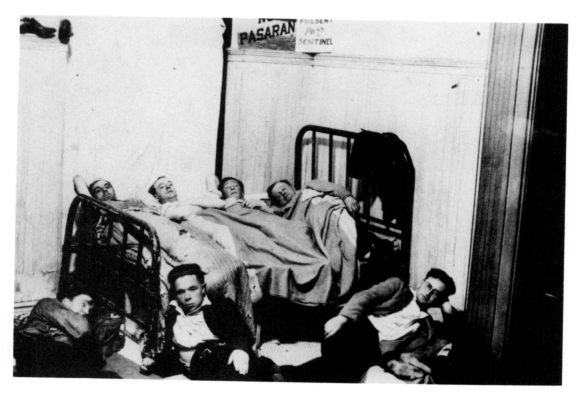

The success of this program convinced King that he could win the election and led him to decide to call it in the summer of 1930. Another factor, less rational perhaps, was the advice he received from a medium in Kingston, a Mrs. Bleaney. The seer had been correct in earlier predictions in 1925 and 1926, and she told the Prime Minister that he would emerge stronger than ever from an election whether held in 1930 or 1931. On balance, she said, 1930 might be more propitious. King, like many of the most famous people of his era, constantly dabbled in spiritualism, and his diary contains detailed accounts of seances, including conversations with Gladstone, Laurier, assorted departed monarchs, and his many relatives. At times, King became near-obsessed with the other world as he sought to reconcile science and religion in a fashion that made sense to him. But never did King let the beyond guide his political life; he was most likely to believe in the advice transmitted through a medium when it accorded with his own shrewd political assessments. In the early months of 1930, politics seemed to agree with the spirits, and the election was set for July 28.

The election campaign did nothing to reduce King's confidence. The crowds everywhere were large, and over radio, used for the first time in an extensive way in this election, his voice projected well. Of course he had hecklers, especially in the West where unemployment was becoming serious; however, the crowds were generally respectful, although Bennett certainly was not. The Tory leader promised to blast Canada's way into the markets of the world, and he preached the doctrine of "Canada First," a policy that curiously for a leader of the Conservative Party threatened to hit out at British trade where it undercut Canadian production. Bennett's assaults soon put Mackenzie King on the defensive, and he found himself forced to respond to the Conservative's attacks. Some of the provincial premiers, notably Howard Ferguson of Ontario and Simon Tolmie of British Columbia, gave King trouble as well, as they harangued him for more money and autonomy for their provinces. Only two provinces had Liberal governments in 1930, a sign of the impending change at Ottawa.

And change there was. The results of the election shook King. The Sunday before the vote he still expected a sweep, a small sweep. "The lessened prosperity and the way it has been played up is all I fear, — but my faith is stronger and I believe we will win with a good majority." The results devastated him, for the Liberals elected only 90 members against

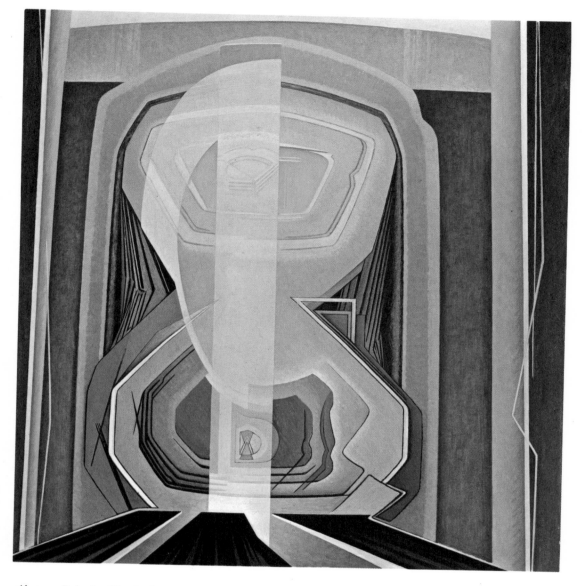

Abstract Painting No. 20, by Lawren
Harris.
*The National Gallery of Canada,
Ottawa.*

138 Conservatives. Farmer labour groups and independents added 17 more to bring the new Parliament to its full complement. King had been whipped, even in Quebec where the Conservatives won 25 seats, even on the Prairies where the Conservatives won 23. King had been defeated, but he consoled himself with this thought in his diary:

> I have gone down if I have with flying colours. A fine record of Govt., a fine issue etc. & before more difficult times come. It looks as tho' it means Bennett for a while then a Liberal party with a long lease of power later on. . . . I believe it is all for the best & only pray for God to give me strength & vision.

To Bennett would fall the job of dealing with the worst of the Great Depression, and King was almost lucky in the way he lost power at the time he did. Not that this had been the Liberal leader's wish, not at all. Power was to secure and to hold, but God moved in mysterious ways, and King was certain that "it was all for the best."

For the people it was the worst of times. The Depression gathered momentum as time passed, and its effects were profound. Unemployment spread through the land, rising from 116,000 in 1929 to 371,000 in 1930 to 481,000 in 1931, 741,000 in 1932, and 826,000 in 1933, the very bottom of the slump. Those figures were untrustworthy, essentially including only those reported without work and excluding many thousands riding the freights from town to town and many ot the dispossessed middle class who were too proud to register. In addition, those unemployment figures, high enough as they were, did not include dependents. A married man without work put his wife and two, three, or more children on welfare with him. Probably between 26 and 33 per cent were out of work in 1933 with as many as 2,000,000 of the labour force dependent for survival on such aid as the state and private charity could give.

Relief was so shattering an experience that many people avoided it by desperate means. To be on relief meant to be at the mercy of petty bureaucrats who could not escape the belief that they had a job because they were virtuous compared with those who did not. It meant doing useless work because penny-pinching city councils insisted that no one had the right to anything for free. Men sawed wood by hand rather than by using a power saw; others picked weeds or dug ditches and filled them in. "It was all justified," one middle-class relief

The relief camp at Barriefield, Ontario, one of
a series built across the country to accom-
modate and assist the unemployed during the
Depression.
Public Archives Canada, PA-35576.

Interior of the main sleeping hut in the relief
camp at the air station in Ottawa.
Public Archives Canada, C-31058.

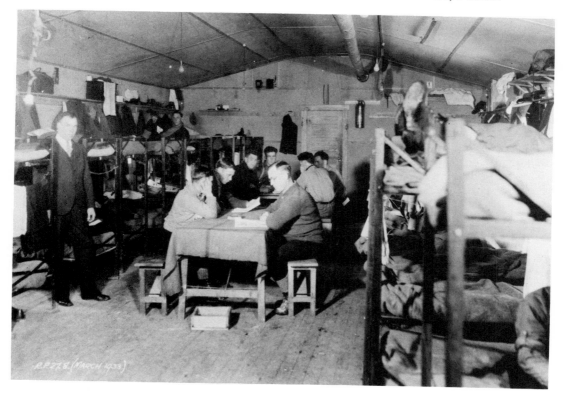

The Depression had a devastating effect on the morale of many of the unemployed, particularly the older single men. Bread and a stew seem to have been served in this spartan relief centre.
Miller Services.

recipient remembered of Winnipeg, "on the grounds that the exercise would be good for us, that working would improve our morale, and that, by providing us with a token opportunity to work for our relief, we would be freed of the stigma of accepting charity." But nothing worked. "The fatuous nature of the projects the authorities invented quickly brought the entire makework concept into disrepute."

The shortage of money threw family budgets out the window, and inevitably the health of a generation suffered. In Montreal, the Federated Agencies, a collection of charitable groups, recommended this as the Sunday menu for relief recipients:

Breakfast   Rolled Oats or Cracked Wheat
Molasses
Bread and Butter
Milk

Lunch	Sliced Meat
	Tomato Sauce
	Onion, Potato or [Stew with Dumplings]
	Bread and Butter
Supper	Chopped Raw Cabbage
	Grated Raw Carrot or Cheese Sauce on Toast
	Hot Water Gingerbread
	Milk

Sunday's menu was the best of the week, of course, and many of the relief families made do without the suggested sliced meat at lunch time.

On the Prairies, the great granary of Canada, the situation was still worse. The West was hit by drought, by grasshoppers, by windstorms that blew away the top soil. The devastation was near total and it went on and on. Production was low, but prices were lower still, and farmers could not even recover the cost of seed from an acre's produce. In December 1932, No. 1 Northern wheat sold at 42¢ a bushel, the lowest price in centuries. The dust was everywhere, the grasshoppers ate whatever grain could emerge from the tortured soil, and the

Coinciding with the Depression, years of drought brought desolation to large areas in the southern Prairies. Photographs can only suggest rather than depict the result. This abandoned farmhouse, surrounded by drifted soil, was south of Swift Current, Saskatchewan. *Saskatchewan Archives Photograph.*

Strikers from unemployment camps in the West riding the rails to Ottawa in a protest "march" in June 1935. The unemployed were a constant worry to the railways, for they infested freight trains (especially those bound for the milder climate of the West Coast) and often travelled under extremely hazardous conditions. *Public Archives Canada, C-29399.*

markets were non-existent. "We were all poverty stricken . . . in our district," one farmer in Camrose, Alberta, remembered,

> even though we had good land and most of us had worked hard. We didn't have to wear gunny sacking for clothing and eat gophers as they did down in the dried-out Youngstown area. But I had neighbours who were living on skimmed milk and potatoes. The telephones were taken from one farm home after another, until we were finally the only farm with a telephone. . . . The poverty was incredible.

Another Albertan, a bailiff, recalled evicting the farmers from their land:

> The winter of 1932 was grim and tough. Eggs were five cents a dozen; hogs two cents a pound; cattle around five or six

cents a pound. There was great pressure put on by creditors to collect debts for land and machinery. The situation grew desperate in 1933. Evictions for nonpayment of debts began to take place. I had to go . . . to give a family the bad news that they were to be evicted immediately. On this farm a man and his wife, three or four children, and a bed-ridden mother-in-law lived in an old shack. I had to tell that middle-aged man and his fragile wife, "My instructions are to put you on the road allowance at once." Another time I had to seize all a man's furniture. This man lived in a poor shack on a farm with his wife and children. He owed money for the furniture. . . . The furniture was removed. (Both men are quoted by J. A. Irving in *The Social Credit Movement in Alberta*, University of Toronto Press.)

The Canadian economy had virtually ground to a halt. The Gross National Product plummeted, falling by 1933 to $3.5 billion, not quite 60 per cent of what it had been in 1929. Newsprint production, along with wheat one of the basic staples of Canada's export market, fell sharply. So did world prices for minerals, another of Canada's longtime money makers, dropping in total value of exports by more than half from 1929 to 1932. Worse, production was inequitably distributed across the country. In the Prairies, personal income was reduced by two-thirds or more, while in manufacturing

A "Bennett buggy" in northern Alberta in the 1930s. The famous Model-T Ford had the great advantage of being light in weight: when neither repairs nor gasoline could be paid for, it could be hauled by horses, or (as in this extreme case) by oxen. *Glenbow-Alberta Institute, Calgary, Alberta.*

Ontario the decline was about one-third, severe enough but a far cry from the Western disaster. Nor was everyone poor. For a man on salary, the Depression was not a terrible experience providing he kept his job. Prices for food and services dropped substantially — the index fell from 121.6 in 1929 to 94.3 in 1933 — and the Depression meant that young girls could be hired for next to nothing as domestics. Of course, the surplus of labour, a polite euphemism for the thousands of unemployed, meant that jobs were filled by people who were grateful for any salary at all. At the Robert Simpson Co. in Toronto, women worked as clerks for $5 for a five and a half-day week. Even with low prices, $5 did not go very far.

Profits fell too. The Depression forced many small firms under and tended to reinforce the trend to consolidation, for only the large firms could tighten their corporate belts and struggle through the worst years of the decade. In 1929, reported corporation profits before taxes were $396 million; in 1932, there was a reported loss of $98 million. But from then on the Depression profit picture brightened for business as labour costs, almost always the largest portion of costs, remained low.

Reported Corporation Profits

1929	$396,000,000
1933	73,000,000
1934	191,000,000
1935	237,000,000
1936	314,000,000
1937	432,000,000
1938	334,000,000
1939	521,000,000

The Depression gave some firms a chance to prosper and expand by feeding off the weaker concerns. In Toronto and Montreal, the large department stores contracted for clothing at such low prices that their contractors, desperate for any orders at all, were obliged to cut wages drastically. In Montreal, for example, men in the clothing industry were working for as little as 10¢ an hour while women earned only 8 or 9¢ an hour. And there was no redress. The authors of a report on employment conditions in the clothing industry reported that "the workers were powerless to complain. Terrified by the danger of losing their jobs, they dared not ask concessions that might lose them favour with 'the boss' . . ."

But not everyone was hurting. The Royal Winter Fair in

Toronto continued to draw the social elite of Southern Ontario to the horse shows, and the social pages were full of the doings of the important and influential. "Nobody thought about money in those days," John David Eaton, the heir to the great Eaton's fortune remembered, "because they never saw any. You could take your girl to a supper dance at the hotel for $10, and that included the bottle and a room for you and your friends to drink it in. I'm glad I grew up then. It was a good time for everybody. People learned what it means to work."

That was the problem, graphically recalled. A gap separated the perceptions of those with a job and money as well as those in the middle and upper classes from those dispossessed and on the dole. If a man had a job, he was convinced it was because of his virtuous hard work; if he was unemployed, it was a reflection on his manhood and a crushing blow to his status. The psychic costs of the Depression were enormous, but to politicians, almost all from the professions and the middle class, none of this was apparent. Certainly the Members of Parliament in Ottawa knew of the privation of the "dirty thirties"; certainly they sympathized and gave to charity. But they could not conceive what it meant to be on relief or to see your children waste away. They could not know because they failed to experience the rigors of the Depression; they could not know because they could not understand.

Within his limitations, Prime Minister Bennett tried to understand. Six weeks after his election to office in the July general election, Bennett called Parliament into session in an effort to honour his promises of rapid action. Action there was. The House of Commons voted $20 million for unemployment relief and public works, a very large sum compared to a federal budget of $400 million in the last year of good times. The tariff was hiked sharply, an effort to protect the home market against cheap imports and the dumping of foreign goods into Canada. Later that year, at an Imperial Conference in London, he tried to persuade the British to agree that if Canada raised its general tariff by ten per cent, it would be a benefit to British goods that would enter the Dominion at the old rates. London was not impressed with Mr. Bennett, nor did they admire his style two years later when an Imperial Economic Conference met at Ottawa. The results of the 1932 conference were the Ottawa agreements, a set of tariff changes that gave Canadian producers minor benefits in the British market in return for a general rise in the Canadian tariff, much as the Prime Minister had proposed at the 1930 meetings. Cer-

The opening of the Maple Leaf Gardens in Toronto in 1932. Construction of this famous arena during the Depression was an act of faith on the part of a leading sports figure, C. F. C. (Conn) Smythe. He and others bought the Toronto St. Pats hockey club, renamed it the Maple Leafs, and built the Gardens to be its home base. *Alexandra Studio*.

tainly Canada had not succeeded in blasting her way into the markets of the world — raising tariffs, on the contrary, tended to reduce world trade.

Other than these attempts to alter the unalterable state of the Dominion's economy, Bennett did little. He had tried to help the unemployed by pouring millions of dollars of aid — $255 million between 1930 and 1935 — into a bottomless barrel; he had tried to stimulate production by raising the tariff. If neither method worked — and neither did — then he was stumped. Slumps were supposed to be temporary and the tariff in the past had always been the right tool to cushion the economy from the worst effects of depression. But in the 1930s nothing worked the way it was supposed to, nothing at all. The Depression grew worse until by 1933 it reached its very nadir.

Bennett was completely perplexed by his inability to deal successfully with the nation's problems. A businessman, he thought in direct and simple terms. Clearly, saboteurs among the people, reds, radicals, socialists, were spoiling his efforts. A victim of his own and his class's limitations, Bennett began to preach patience to the people at the same time that he moved to crush radicalism in the country. The reds had to be crushed under "the iron heel of capitalism," he said in a devastatingly ill-chosen phrase, and he moved to deport troublemakers. In 1929 only 1964 people had been deported from the country, but in 1931 that figure increased by three-and-a-half times to 6583 and in the next year it rose again to 7647. Agitators were shipped out of Canada, along with those immigrants who were unfortunate enough to find themselves public charges. On another occasion, a delegation of unemployed was met in 1932 by armed RCMP troopers on Parliament Hill, and opposition to the policies of the Prime Minister began gradually to be equated with opposition to the system or the state. This use of force frightened many Canadians, and C. G. Power, an independent-minded Liberal MP from Quebec City, expressed the feelings of many when he said in a speech in Parliament that Bennett was "as inconstant as it is possible to be, that he is variable, that he is unstable, that he lacks in character that ponderation, that prudence and that wisdom that mark a truly great statesman." Power added that "in his public relations," Bennett "often exhibits the manners of a Chicago policeman, and the temperament of a Hollywood actor."

Bennett also ran into difficulty when in 1932 it was revealed that the millionaire Prime Minister kept a suite of 17 rooms at the Chateau Laurier Hotel in Ottawa for which he paid only $400 a month. The hotel was run by the Canadian National Railways, a government-owned concern, and in evidence before a Parliamentary Committee the President of the railway indicated that $110,000 in renovations had been made to the suite. When Bennett was asked in Committee if he thought 75¢ a day for a room was reasonable, he could reply only that he paid what he was asked to pay.

The sting for Bennett was eased somewhat by Mackenzie King's own difficulties during the period, for Mr. King was involved in the one episode in his career where scandal was attached to his name. The investigations of a parliamentary committee in 1931 revealed that a group of promoters who had been the beneficiaries of the King government's award of authorization to divert St. Lawrence River water for hydro purposes had been exceedingly generous contributors to the Liberal party in the 1930 campaign. The sum of $600,000 to $700,000 was admitted to by one executive of Beauharnois

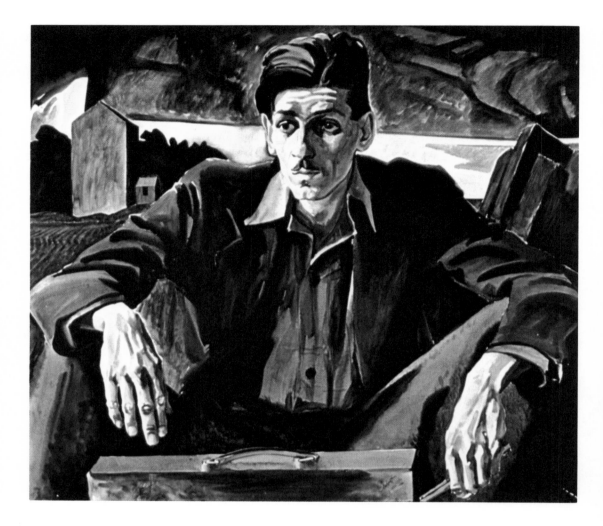

Young Canadian, by Charles Comfort,
O.C., R.C.A.
Hart House, University of Toronto.
Charles Comfort's striking portrait of
a young Canadian caught in the depths
of the Depression: "Great hands ready
to work but little work to be done."

Power, who offered in explanation, "Gratefulness was always regarded as an important factor in dealing with democratic governments." Indeed. But if this was not bad enough, the investigation showed that Mackenzie King while Prime Minister had gone to Bermuda for a holiday; on this trip his hotel expenses had been paid by the Beauharnois company. Like the Prime Minister, King found himself in difficulty because of a few hundred dollars in hotel bills. To King, this was probably the most trying period of his life. And in a long, laboured speech in Parliament on July 30, 1931, he admitted:

> Individual members of the Liberal party may have done what they should not have done. The party is not thereby disgraced. The party is not disgraced but it is in the valley of humiliation. I tell the people of this country today that as its leader I feel humiliated. . . . But we are going to come out of the valley, not in any boasting way but with a determination to see to it that so far as the cause of Liberalism in this country is concerned, it will advance to higher and stronger and better ground than it ever has occupied in the past.

If by that King meant that when he was in power again he would reform the financing of politics, he was speaking only for the moment and not for posterity. Party finance remains an area of mystery, confusion, and justified suspicion.

More recently, at the beginning of 1977, accusations were made that King took bribes and "was on the take until the day he died," a charge based on check stubs and deposit slips uncovered in the Public Archives of Canada in Ottawa. In fact, King took no bribes. What he did do was to become the grateful recipient of the principal and interest of a trust fund set up for him by wealthy friends across the country. The money was intended to restore and maintain Laurier House, the Ottawa residence King had inherited from Lady Laurier, and to relieve the Prime Minister of financial worries. This it did, but the whole affair smacks too much of corruption, of too-close links between the rich and the government. About all one can say in King's defence is that other Prime Ministers and Leaders of the Opposition since his time have had similar funds raised for them.

In policy terms, Mackenzie King's spell in the Opposition was no more fruitful. An Opposition leader's role was to oppose and King and his party did this job, attacking the government for all its sins of omission and commission, but proposing very few positive remedies of their own. It was always very difficult to bring a polyglot Liberal party to consensus on major issues, and therefore it was best to keep policies hazy and fuzzy, to remain undefined and free. Clearly, the Depression continued to control events, and so long as it did Bennett was doomed. King convinced himself — and correctly — that he need do nothing but allow Bennett enough rope to hang himself, his party, and his government for a generation.

Other Canadians were not prepared to sit on their hands and do nothing while hundreds of thousands suffered in the midst of economic collapse. The Communists were busy organizing the unemployed and staging rallies that were brutally repressed, thus making more revolutionaries out of ordinary men and women. More important, a genuine social democratic

J. S. Woodsworth, founder of the Co-operative Commonwealth Federation, the CCF, now the New Democratic Party. Though many disagreed with his opinions, few members of the House of Commons have won such universal respect.
Public Archives Canada, C-34443.

Delegates to the founding conference of the
CCF, held in Regina in July 1933. J. S. Woods-
worth is seated in the middle of the front row.
Public Archives Canada, C-29298.

A CCF picnic held in
Wascana Park, Regina, in
the early 1930s. The CCF
often convened their
meetings in the form of
picnics, like the one
pictured here.
*Public Archives Canada,
C-29310.*

Lazare, by Jean-Paul
Lemieux, 1941.
Art Gallery of Ontario.

party was created at Regina in the summer of 1933. The Co-operative Commonwealth Federation was a grouping of remnants of the Progressives, of labour leaders, and of urban intellectuals deeply affected by British Fabian socialism, and it brought a new spirit into Canadian politics. Its manifesto, drafted at the Regina meeting, called for a new social order that would replace the profit system of capitalism by a socialist state in which government planning would be the order of the day. Economic equality, social justice, collective bargaining, unemployment insurance — the list of firm positions went on. And for its leader the CCF had an able and saintly man in J. S. Woodsworth. A minister, Woodsworth had become disillusioned with the church during the Great War and he had turned to more direct action to change the social order. In 1919 he was arrested during the Winnipeg Strike for printing verses from the Gospels in the strikers' newspaper; soon after his release he ran for the House of Commons on a Labour ticket in North Winnipeg. Elected again and again, Woodsworth acquired a great reputation in the House and in the country as a spokesman for social justice and good sense, and he would lay the groundwork for the later growth of the CCF.

If the Cooperative Commonwealth Federation was one response to the Depression, Social Credit was another. Like

William Aberhart, the schoolteacher-evangelist who turned to politics and led the Social Credit Party in Alberta to its astonishing electoral victory in 1935. He was premier of the province until his death in 1943.
Public Archives Canada, C-16476.

the CCF, its ideological roots were in the West and in British political thought. The founder and inventor of Social Credit's monetary theories was a Britisher, Major C. H. Douglas. According to the Major, the total of all purchasing power was inevitably lower than the total price of all the goods produced by modern technology. The result was poverty in the midst of plenty. The answer, Social Credit theory proclaimed, lay in creating enough money to bring purchasing power and the total cost of goods into line. This new money would be distributed directly to the people by government in the form of dividends. Unfortunately, in addition to this relatively harmless and even beguiling theory, British Social Credit carried with it overtones of anti-Semitism and fascist paramilitarism, some of its followers even affecting uniforms.

The ideology of Social Credit found its way to Alberta where it fell into the hands of one of the most extraordinary political figures in Canadian history, William Aberhart. A high school principal in Calgary turned radio evangelist, Aberhart was a plumpish and rather pop-eyed man who would have been destroyed by television. But on radio he was brilliant, and his evangelical broadcasts captured enormous audiences in the 1920s and 1930s. When Social Credit theory began to make its way into his religious speeches on the air and, when Social Credit Clubs began to spring up across the province, it was clear that a political movement was in the making. In Alberta the time was ripe. The province had been devastated by the Crash, and the old party system had never been strong there since the Great War. The government in power, controlled by the United Farmers of Alberta, was old, tired, and discredited, and Aberhart swept it out like dust. His program was Social Credit and its remedies for the Depression:

> What is the remedy? . . . Social Credit with its basic dividend of $25.00 per month starts out with the corrective measures at once. It places purchasing power in the hands of the consumer. . . . Where does all the money come from? We don't use money. Then where does all the credit come from? Why, out of the end of a fountain pen.

This gospel of inflation and easy money was obviously attractive to a society that was flat on its back, and Aberhart was elected in 1935 with 56 of 63 seats in the Alberta legislature.

The faithful who had found their new Messiah in the radio preacher–school principal would be disappointed. In power, Aberhart turned out to be almost as cautious as the representatives of the old parties that he scorned. The dividend was not paid, and whenever the Premier was pressed by his followers to implement the fundamental tenets of Social Credit theory, the British North America Act interfered. But the lack of provincial powers vital to enacting Social Credit theory was advantageous to Aberhart, for he could blame Ottawa, the East, the vested interests for his inability to change the financial system. The war and the subsequent discovery of billions of barrels of oil would eventually bring prosperity to Alberta, and Social Credit would be then revealed as small-c conservatism in a new guise.

The federal election of 1935 brought the CCF and Social Credit into the national political arena, as well as another grouping, the Reconstruction Party. Reconstruction was led by Harry Stevens, a British Columbia Tory who had been one of the leading figures in the Bennett Cabinet until he split with the Prime Minister in 1934. Stevens saw himself as the representative and protector of small businesses, and he tried through an investigation into price spreads to expose the efforts of the great corporations to drive small firms under. For a time he was supported by Bennett, but the Prime Minister was not a man to tolerate another loud horn player in what he saw as his own one-man band. Stevens was allowed to leave the party, to form his own grouping, and to steal hundreds of thousands of votes away from Conservative candidates.

But Bennett had his own surprises in store. In January 1935 he began a series of radio pronouncements across a national network. The speeches soon became known as the "New Deal," a direct comparison with the program of policies implemented since 1933 by President Franklin Roosevelt in the United States. Bennett's New Deal speeches represented a major change in his style and rhetoric. Instead of attacking the radicals who threatened the established order, Bennett now attacked the capitalists who were the major beneficiaries of it.

"The time has come," the Prime Minister told his radio audience on January 2, 1935, "when I must speak to you with the utmost frankness about our national affairs." In this way began one of the more extraordinary deathbed conversions in Canadian politics. "If you believe that things should be left as they are, you and I hold contrary and irreconcilable views. I am for reform," Bennett said. Over the course of the next few addresses the Prime Minister spelled out a series of promises for minimum wage acts, for aid to farmers, for a new and better old-age pensions act, for "fair play between the producer and the consumer, between industry and the public." The fourth address, delivered on January 9, was probably the most hard-hitting:

> Selfish men, and this country is not without them — men whose mounting bank rolls loom larger than your happiness, corporations without souls and without virtue — these, fearful that this Government might impinge on what they have grown to regard as their immemorial right of exploitation, will whisper against us. They will call us radicals.
>
> They will say that this is the first step on the road to socialism. We fear them not. . . . I think if they are sensible, they will agree that it is more in their interests than ours, that they should cooperate with us in our just purpose.

Bennett's speeches had been made without being canvassed beforehand in the cabinet, and some ministers were stunned by what their chief had done.

But Bennett soon proceeded to introduce his proposals into Parliament in the form of a series of acts: The Employment and Social Insurance Act, The Dominion Trade and Industry Commission Act, The Minimum Wages Act, The Weekly Day of Rest Act, The Eight Hour Day Act, The Farmers' Creditors Arrangement Act, The Natural Products Marketing Act, and on and on. The proposals by no means amounted to a revolution, but to many in big business they were frightening examples of the way politicians, even those believed to be "safe," could be swung from their moorings by electoral pressures. To those on the left, the Bennett New Deal was good as far as it went, but the package did not go far enough. To Mackenzie King and the Liberals, the New Deal was a matter that demanded careful study, considered judgment, and calm thought. Probably it was unconstitutional; certainly it was politically dangerous. Mr. King said little of substance about the New Deal.

In fact King's campaign in the fall of 1935 was devoted to saying little of substance. With unemployment still high, with the Depression's grip still firm (although the period since 1933 had been one of a gradual upturn), why say anything? The Liberal slogan was "King or Chaos," a neat phrase that expressed the Liberals' fundamental belief in order. The radical parties of right and left were dangers, Liberals said, the CCF as much as Social Credit. Stevens could not win and the Bennett government for five years had demonstrated its

inability to govern and to meet the needs of the country. In 1935, these bromides still sounded fresh, and the electorate responded to the Liberal party. Big business, frightened by the Conservatives, eventually swung its support to Mackenzie King and showered him with money in campaign donations, and Bennett's Conservatives and the New Deal went down to defeat before the power of the *status quo*. The Liberals elected 178 MPs, the largest majority to that time, and they managed this with only 44.8 per cent of the popular vote. The new parties on left and right had stolen votes away from the old parties, but the Liberals had still received the largest popular vote. Bennett's New Deal was left in ruins by the electorate, and the Tories returned a bare 40 members, 25 of them from Ontario. Social Credit received 4.1 per cent of the popular vote, but this was largely concentrated in Alberta where

King electioneering in Brampton, Ontario.
Ontario Archives, 3117 #4.

A glimpse of Mackenzie
King campaigning shortly
before the general election
of 1935, which returned
the Liberals to power.
*Public Archives Canada,
C-13261.*

Les cartes sont mélangées

Bourgeois, 1935

La Presse, Montreal

— Moi, j'ai quatre as!
— Moi, aussi!
— Moi, aussi!
— Moi, de même!

Bourgeois, cartoonist for
La Presse, Montreal, pokes
fun at the four party
leaders in the election of
1935. King, Bennett,
Stevens (of the short-lived
Reconstruction Party),
and Woodsworth all claim
to be holding four aces.
*Metropolitan Toronto
Library Board.*

Aberhart's disciples won 15 seats. The CCF, which polled 387,000 votes in this its first try at the polls, won only 7 seats, but Harry Stevens' Reconstruction Party, with 384,000 votes, managed to take only one seat, Stevens' own. The public had been told that the choice was King or Chaos. In October 1935 they had Mackenzie King.

The Depression had not changed the Liberal leader's perceptions of his role or of the role of government. The task

The Cabinet in 1930: Mackenzie King and his ministers in the historic Cabinet Room in the East Block of the Parliament Buildings.
Public Archives Canada, C-9332.

of government was to keep taxes low, to reduce government spending to the minimum, and to facilitate the flow of trade within the country and abroad. One of Mackenzie King's first acts in office was to pick up where Bennett's administration had left off and to negotiate a new and freer trade arrangement with the United States. A further agreement was signed with the Roosevelt government in 1938. The government also introduced measures to assist Prairie farmers, hard hit by the weather conditions and crop failures of the past years. The Minister of Agriculture, J. G. Gardiner, the former Saskatchewan Premier, was particularly and properly sensitive to the needs of his region, and the Prairie Farm Rehabilitation Act, a piece of Bennett's 1935 legislation, became his vehicle. Through amendments, the PFRA gradually became an important tool in improving agricultural methods on the dry lands of the Prairies, producing crops that were far more resistant to the vagaries of weather.

Unemployment was still the major national problem when King resumed office, and shortly after the election he named a National Employment Commission to reorganize relief expenditures and to recommend measures that would create employment. The Commission would soon bring in its report, the first piece of modern planning the Dominion had seen. To the Commission, problems were nationwide in scope and had to be considered in this light. The federal government had to recognize that it had the responsibility to keep the nation's economy moving; thus, employment and unemployment both were national concerns. The Dominion should assume the responsibility for the costs of unemployment relief, the Commission recommended, a far different system from the existing patchwork of federal grants, provincial administration, and municipal confusion. In addition, and more radically still, the Commission urged that increased federal expenditures be pumped into the economy in times of economic depression. This was a very new idea in the mid-1930s, a product of the economic theorizing of the British economist John Maynard Keynes, and something fairly similar to the economic policies that Professor Alvin Hansen and others had been suggesting to Roosevelt in the United States. Keynesian economics stood the world on its end, flying in the face of the conventional wisdom that balanced budgets were the key to sound growth and fiscal stability.

Mr. King, an economist by training, was very much a proponent of sound economics. To him the balanced budget had status almost as an article of faith. But to his shock, several of his ministers had come to the conclusion that moderate Keynesianism and the recommendations of the National Employment Commission were correct for the circumstances. After the Minister of Labour, Norman Rogers, threatened to resign if changes were not made, King gave in. The budget of 1938 was the first, as King's biographer, H. Blair Neatby, says, in which a government "consciously decided to spend money to counteract a low in the business cycle." In addition, taxes were lowered and tax exemptions for private investors were offered, a deliberate attempt to encourage the spending of money in the hope that money spent would multiply its effects throughout the economy. No immediate effect came of this tentative tinkering: the sums involved were too small to turn around a whole economy. But the precedent of intervention had been set; it would become the rule thereafter.

Another area in which King moved was toward a form of unemployment insurance. King basically favoured such a scheme, but as always caution dominated. In addition, to implement such a measure would require cooperation with the provinces to secure an amendment to the British North America Act. King was agreeable, but the provinces were not. Jealous of their powers, Ontario and Quebec resisted any efforts by Ottawa to horn into their jurisdiction, and the Unemployment Insurance Act would not finally become law until the summer of 1940 when the war had already gone some distance to ending unemployment.

The provinces also questioned another King initiative, the establishment of the Royal Commission on Dominion-Provincial Relations. Appointed on August 14, 1937, the Royal Commission was charged with examining the constitutional allocation of revenues between Ottawa and the provinces and studying the federal subsidies paid to the provinces. For the relatively rich provinces of British Columbia and Ontario, any such Royal Commission would inevitably cost them money and had therefore to be opposed. For Quebec, such a study was a threat to provincial autonomy; for Alberta a commission of this type was probably a violation of Social Credit theory. But for the other provinces, desperately short of money and burdened with debt, anything that promised the possibility of more money had to be a good thing.

The provincial premiers all faced difficulties in the Depression. Some found their treasuries empty and their relief costs enormous; others felt threatened by the radicalism that was

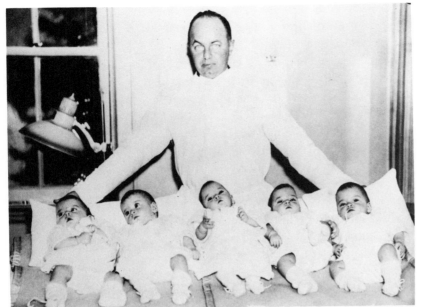

Hepburn with the famous Dionne quintuplets, born at Callandar, Ontario, in May 1934. Hepburn had become premier of Ontario six weeks after their birth. *Public Archives Canada, C-19533.*

Maurice Duplessis (left), Premier of Quebec, and Mitchell Hepburn, Premier of Ontario, two political thorns in Mackenzie King's side, photographed together in an amiable and informal moment. *Public Archives Canada, C-19518.*

latent in the events of the period. The two most interesting premiers were very different men, united by only two things — their desire to preserve and extend the autonomy of their governments and their dislike for Mackenzie King. Mitchell Hepburn, elected in 1934 in Ontario, was nominally a Liberal, nominally a supporter of his federal leader. But King was slightly frightened by the Premier's raffishness, his demagoguery, and worried about his cronies who were men of wealth and power with their own axes to grind. Disputes about patronage, power exports, and provincial rights brought relations between the two to an end by 1937-38.

Hepburn's response to labour trouble in Ontario exacerbated the situation even more. The Congress of Industrial Organizations came to Oshawa in 1937 and set out to organize the General Motors Company plant there. To Hepburn, the CIO was a foreign agitators' gang, a bunch of reds who threatened the stability of Ontario and who incidentally posed a threat to the mining interests of Hepburn's wealthy cronies. The Premier set out to crush the CIO incursion, and he mobilized the press, the police, and the public behind him. In the end, Hepburn was only partially successful in his aim, but he had increased his resentment for the federal government substantially, a direct response to Ottawa's unwillingness to give him RCMP reinforcements to preserve "order" in Oshawa. The net result of Oshawa when added to the other Ottawa-Toronto disputes was that the federal Liberal party was forced to set up its own organization in Ontario: Hepburn had seceded from the Liberal party.

The Quebec scene, where Maurice Duplessis held power, was even more difficult. Duplessis had been a Conservative until he joined with disaffected Liberals in an effort to topple the *ancien régime* of corrupt Liberals who had ruled the province for a generation. The Union Nationale soared to power in 1936, only to see Duplessis drive out all who were not personally loyal to him. The resulting regime closely resembled the old one in effect, except that Duplessis strongly advocated more autonomy for Quebec. For Duplessis too, Mackenzie King was the enemy to be destroyed.

The political scene, then, was volatile. Men like Duplessis and Hepburn were able demagogues who had been elected because they seemed different from the governments that had brought on the Depression; in office, however, they proved to be no different. For Mackenzie King, compliant provinces that accepted Ottawa's power calmly were better than fractious ones, but the situation had to be dealt with as it existed. In any case, the Liberal party was strong federally in both of the central Canadian provinces — and elsewhere, too.

But by the end of the 1930s, those federal-provincial quarrels were suddenly dwarfed by events abroad. The rise of Hitler, the resurgence of German power, and the series of German diplomatic and military triumphs in Central Europe brought the world to the brink of war once more, just a quarter century after the beginning of "the war to end wars."

5

Canada in the World, 1920-39

THE THREAT OF WAR IN EUROPE IN 1938 and 1939 dominated official concerns in Ottawa as it did everywhere. The Great War had been so destructive in human, material, and moral terms that every sensible person feared a new war. For Mackenzie King, a man of peace, war in Europe threatened the fragile unity of Canada as no other issue could. By bringing the questions of imperialism and nationalism to the fore, war would again divide English Canadians, anxious to aid the Mother Country, from French Canadians, convinced that Canada's duty was simply to defend itself. War would upset King's long, slow, calculated advance to a more independent policy; it would divide the country; it could destroy the Liberal party.

King's policies had been geared to avoid these eventualities from the day he took power for the first time in 1921. The nation's international *persona* was far different than it had been at the beginning of the Great War. The Borden government's participation in the Imperial War Conferences of 1917 and after had built on Canada's war service to win advanced status. This new status had been recognized in the peace treaties and by Canadian representation as a separate state in the League of Nations. But the war's achievements for Canadian status were seen by many as too small a prize, too unimportant a reward, for 60,000 dead in combat. In Quebec especially, this new status meant nothing, for Canada was still too tightly bound to Britain for the average *Québécois* to be happy.

King could see this burgeoning isolationism in Canada and in the United States. He did not share it personally, and he was a firm and constant devotee of the British connection. Royalty mattered to him, dukes and duchesses and marquesses

Dr. O. D. Skelton. Skelton was Under Secretary of State for External Affairs from 1925 until his sudden death early in 1941. Norman Robertson succeeded him in that post and he was succeeded in turn by Lester B. Pearson in 1946. These three were principal advisers to Mackenzie King on external affairs for all but his first few years as prime minister. *Public Archives Canada, C-2089.*

and countesses always ranked as important persons in his eyes. But British policy was something very different than Britons. British policy, to Mackenzie King, was at once bungling and cunning. The British would probably make a mess of international politics, but he feared they would nonetheless seek to find some way of associating Canada with them in their errors. The task for Canada under his leadership, therefore, was to end the *de facto* diplomatic unity of the Empire so that Canada would not be lumped in with British positions in foreign policy.

Did this mean that there would be a distinctive Canadian position? Not really. Mackenzie King's view of foreign policy was much like Sir Wilfrid Laurier's before him. External questions were important, yes, but it was more important that Canada should develop itself and harvest its resources. Energy would be wasted abroad, particularly when foreign quarrels tended to divide the "two founding races" in Canada. That position was sensible in a world that had not yet been shrunk by advanced communications, and the simple fact was that Canadian interests in the world were strictly limited.

Mackenzie King's first major test in this area came with the Chanak crisis of 1922. Britain found itself embroiled with Turkey in a controversy around the Dardanelles, a controversy that was mainly necessary for British domestic political reasons. The details are immaterial, but Prime Minister David Lloyd George, aided and abetted by Winston Churchill, sent telegrams to the Dominions requesting support and troops, telegrams that were released to the press before they arrived at their destinations. Lloyd George and Company could argue that they assumed the Empire stood as one international person and that it would act as such in a crisis, a not entirely unreasonable assumption considering the gestures in the direction of Empire solidarity that had been made at the Imperial Conference of 1921, a conference that Prime Minister Meighen had attended for Canada. But King was not Meighen, and when reporters told him of the Lloyd George telegram he was horrified. So he stalled. Parliament would have to decide such a question, King said, but fortunately Parliament was not in session. The result was that no Canadian contingent was sent to this non-crisis (for so it proved to be). But Arthur Meighen, much more susceptible to tugs on the Imperial heartstrings, argued that when Britain's call had come Canada should have replied, "Ready, aye, ready." That kind of attitude, that almost unthinking response to British policy right or wrong, was the one that had torn Canada to pieces in 1917. To Mackenzie King, that attitude would not do.

As King told Parliament later, the British request for troops at Chanak was the "first and only intimation . . . received from the British Government" of the crisis. This was no cooperative policy; this was rule by fiat, something that Canadians could not tolerate. Britain had worldwide interests, bases, and investments; Canada had none and thus Canadian policy had to be different. With this assessment of the Canadian position in view, Mackenzie King went to London in 1923 to attend the Imperial Conference.

Laurier had bemoaned the atmosphere of the Conferences years earlier, the constant talk of Empire, Empire, Empire, plus the power of silken dalliance exercised by beautiful aristocrats. King was as susceptible to this kind of distraction as ever Laurier was, but he found the strength to resist. His government had already shaken the diplomatic unity of the Empire by its actions over Chanak, and Canada had signed a treaty on halibut fishing rights with the United States in her own stead, yet another violation of past practices. Now the Imperial Conference would be pressed by Mackenzie King to recognize the new reality. "We believe," King told the Conference,

> that the decision of Great Britain on any important public issue, domestic or foreign, should be made by the people of Britain, their representatives in Parliament, and the Government responsible to that Parliament. So the decision of Canada on any important issue, domestic or foreign, we believe should be made by the people of Canada, their representatives in Parliament, and the Government responsible to that Parliament.

Mackenzie King returning from the Imperial Conference of 1926. With him (left to right) are Senator W. L. McDougald, the ambitious friend who five years later would involve King in the Beauharnois scandal, Ernest Lapointe, leader of the French-Canadian wing of the Liberal Party, and Vincent Massey, soon to be appointed the first Canadian Minister to the United States.
Public Archives Canada, C-9050.

In other words, as a self-governing Dominion, Canada should be able to make its own policy.

The Conference thrashed through a series of problems with King resisting endlessly every British attempt to create a web of unity. "The obstacle," Lord Curzon, the British Foreign Secretary, wrote to his wife, "has been Mackenzie King, the Canadian, who is both obstinate, tiresome and stupid." In the end, the obstinate, tiresome, and stupid Mackenzie King won, and Curzon, one of the most brilliant (if blinkered) men in British politics had been checkmated. The final communiqué of the Conference noted:

> This Conference is a conference of representatives of the several Governments of the Empire; its views and conclusions on Foreign Policy, . . . are necessarily subject to the action of the Governments and Parliaments of the various portions of the Empire, and it trusts that the results of its deliberations will meet with their approval.

The diplomatic unity of the Empire was effectively ended; Canadian autonomy was a recognized fact; and King had scored a great, if somewhat negative, triumph on the international stage.

Thereafter, only the details remained to be clarified. At the Imperial Conference of 1926, King seemed almost a satisfied power, playing a moderating role between the Irish and the South Africans, who were eager for formal statements of autonomy, and the British Government, which was predictably rather slow to learn the lessons of 1923. All that King wanted this time was that the Governor General's role should be carefully and effectively circumscribed so that the Vice-Regal representative would no longer be the channel of diplomatic communication between the United Kingdom government and Canada. This change he won, a development that led to the eventual posting of High Commissioners to Commonwealth capitals. King also came home from London in 1926 with the Conference's statement that attempted to define the position of Britain and the Dominions, a statement that King, always afraid of precise language and the limitations it put on one, was a bit concerned about. The Dominions, the statement read,

are autonomous Communities within the British Empire, equal in status, in no way subordinate one to another in any

Continued on page 116

OVERLEAF Liberal campaign poster, 1935. *Metropolitan Toronto Library Board.*

113

A UNITED CANADA WILL SOLVE YOUR PROBLEMS

VOTE LIBERAL *and get* ACTION

Canadian Painting, 1915-1945

MACKENZIE KING never displayed any marked interest in things artistic, but he cannot have been unaware of the striking developments that took place in Canadian painting during the four decades he was active in public life.

About the time he entered Laurier's cabinet, the intense interest and pride in Canada engendered by a dozen years of unprecedented expansion and prosperity spilled over into the field of art. Canadian artists became absorbed in an effort to

Continued on page 118

Spring Flood, by Tom Thomson, 1915.
Reproduction courtesy of The McMichael Canadian Collection.

aspect of their domestic or external affairs, though united by a common allegiance to the Crown, and freely associated as members of the British Commonwealth of Nations.

This statement would be transformed into legislation in the Statute of Westminster, passed by the Imperial Parliament in 1931. Thereafter, Canada's legal status was clear: it was a self-governing nation, internally and externally, although by choice it remained part of the British Commonwealth and owed allegiance to the British monarch.

Was King's nationalist policy accepted by the people? Probably it was, although very few Canadians concerned themselves with events abroad in a serious way. The government's Department of External Affairs was a tiny operation, although in Dr. Oscar Skelton, the Under Secretary, it had a permanent head of ability and talent. The press paid little attention to questions of external policy, and elections were not usually noted for their discussion of such issues. For Arthur Meighen, however, the leader of a divided Conservative party, such questions mattered. Meighen's great political problem was to get support in Quebec for Conservatism, and his difficulty was to live down his "Ready, aye, ready" remarks of 1922 on top of his conscriptionist past. To the Conservative leader, the proper response was to assure Quebec that the nation would never send troops abroad until the people in an election had given their consent. This was a moderate, if probably unworkable, step, but Quebec did not seem overly impressed by his speech to this effect made at Hamilton in November 1925, while English-language Conservatives raged. What did this mean? the Toronto *Telegram* cried:

> While other parts of the Empire were fighting Canadians would be voting. Bullets flying in the battle front and ballots flying in Canada. Battles with other parts of the Empire participating and stump speeches on the Canadian hustings. A war horror and an election horror as well. . . . His proposal is, of course, foolish and impractical . . . the beginning of the end if not the actual end of Canada's attachment to the British Empire.

Meighen got nowhere with his proposal and after his defeat in the election of 1926 he was finished as Tory leader, replaced the next year by the seemingly more acceptable Bennett. The irony of the situation was that by 1926 when Meighen made his proposal, the Canadian attachment to the

A group at Canada House, London, in 1936. Left to right: (seated) Georges P. Vanier, Secretary to the High Commissioner; Vincent Massey, High Commissioner for Canada in Britain; (standing) Lester B. Pearson, Counsellor; Ross McLean, Attaché.
Public Archives Canada, C-4053.

Empire had already undergone a *de facto* change thanks to Mackenzie King.

In fact, Prime Minister Bennett changed nothing during his period of power from 1930 to 1935. Mackenzie King had named a Minister to Washington in 1926, and Bennett did nothing to alter this step to direct Canadian-American relations, even naming his brother-in-law, W. D. Herridge, to the post in 1931. Bennett accepted the Statute of Westminster in 1931, and he continued the practice of signing treaties established by his predecessor. In most questions of form and practice, nothing differentiated Bennett's policy from Mackenzie King's.

The result was that by the time the world situation began to worsen in the early middle 1930s, Canada had carved out its own niche in the world and in the Empire. The nation was independent in law, if not yet in practice. Canada sat in the League of Nations at Geneva on its own, negotiated its own treaties and signed them, and had full independence in formulating its policies at home and abroad. Canada had no commitments to Britain or to any other power and took no part in British policy-making except where it believed its own interests were at stake, a rare occurrence. This was not a glamorous policy of activism and interest; in fact, it represented nothing so much as a negative policy, a turning away from the world. But in Canadian terms it was necessary and correct,

Continued on page 120

depict Canada. Among others, Tom Thomson took to the wilds and began to record the beauty and immensity of the Canadian landscape. His remarkable painting entitled *Spring Flood* shows how well he succeeded.

Thomson was drowned in 1917, but painters with whom he had been associated formed the famous Group of Seven in 1920. Pictures that came from the brush of one of them, Lawren Harris, will illustrate some of the developments that followed.

Shacks, by Lawren Harris, 1919.
The National Gallery of Canada, Ottawa.

*Afternoon Sun, North
Shore, Lake Superior,* by
Lawren Harris, 1924.
*The National Gallery
of Canada, Ottawa.*

Shacks, painted in 1919, is typical of Harris's city-oriented
pictures before the formation of the Group of Seven. By contrast, *Afternoon Sun, North Shore, Lake Superior*, painted
only five years later, is the work of an artist fascinated by the
Canadian landscape. Its subject — trees silhouetted against a
vista of lake and hills — attracted all the leading members of
the Group of Seven and resulted in the well-known pictures
by Varley, Lismer, Jackson, and MacDonald.

The Group of Seven disbanded in 1933, just as new winds

Continued on page 122

The Spanish Civil War stirred passions throughout the world and hundreds of Canadians went abroad to fight Fascism. Most served in the Mac-Paps (the Mackenzie-Papineau Battalion) or with the Lincoln and Washington Battalion, a largely American unit. These Canadians, photographed in June 1937, were with the Lincolns.
Public Archives Canada, C-74967.

given the splits in the nation and the pressures that the Depression exacerbated.

By 1935, however, when Mackenzie King returned to power, the state of world politics was such that war could be glimpsed on the horizon. In Japan, a militarist regime was seeking to expand Japanese control in China and Manchuria and looking further afield; in Italy, *il Duce*, Benito Mussolini, was in the midst of a war of aggression in Ethiopia; and in Germany, Adolf Hitler and his Nazi party had succeeded in consolidating internal control and were now beginning to eye seriously the German territories lost in the peace of 1919. With these power-hungry men added to the unstable regimes in other parts of Europe, like Spain, Stalin's Soviet Union, and a host of petty dictatorships, the world was ready to explode. The Depression still hung over the globe and weakened the will to resist war in all countries, but especially in Britain, France, the United States, and Canada.

Part of the problem was that many of the press, politicians, business people, and clergy admired the dictatorships and their direct methods. Mussolini had made the trains run on time. Hitler had solved the Jewish question and ended unemployment in Germany, and Stalin's Communist state was better than the evils of unbridled capitalism. The babble of competing ideologies confused the popular mind, and a widespread feeling that the victors of the Great War had been too hard on the vanquished at the Versailles Peace Conference of 1919 helped make the situation ripe for exploitation. The fascist states took advantage of this mood brilliantly, negotiating toughly, mixing force and bluster, and employing new and effective propaganda techniques to win their way. The world was on the road to war once again, and no one knew how to deal with the threat.

The first overt challenge had come from Japan in Manchuria in 1931 and after, a challenge that the League of Nations had simply failed to meet. Canadian opinion had not been very well developed on this subject, but the Canadian representative at the League, the Hon. C. H. Cahan, the Secretary of State in Bennett's government, gave implicit support to Japan's aggression when he pointed out at the 1932 session that China did not exercise effective control in Manchuria and that Japan claimed it was only seeking to protect its interests and rights there. Along with the other members, Canada stood by while parts of China were swallowed whole by the Empire of Japan.

More serious was the Ethiopian affair of 1935, a crisis that came almost at exactly the same time as the general election in Canada. The Bennett government, through its representative at Geneva, supported the League in its efforts to pressure Italy, and gradually the talk at the world organization's headquarters began to move in the direction of sanctions of an economic nature against aggressors. This was dangerous ground for a country like Canada whose policy to the League had largely been based on an acceptance of the body as a "do-gooder" agency, not as an enforcer of peace in a world of unjust boundaries. But under the pressure of events, the government went along despite a substantial feeling in Canada, and particularly in Catholic Quebec, that Italy was merely bringing civilization to the barbarous Ethiopians. After the cautious Mackenzie King had won the election, the Canadian permanent representative in Geneva, Dr. W. A. Riddell, unfortunately — and probably deliberately — misinterpreted his instructions from Ottawa and pressed for the expansion of

Continued on page 124

Composition No. 1, by
Lawren Harris, 1940.
Collection, The Van-
couver Art Gallery.

of change were blowing through the Canadian art world with
increasing force. Painting ceased to be centred primarily on
Canadian themes and responded to the influences of international modern art. Much of it also ceased to be representa-
tional and became abstract, to such a point that it could scarcely
be said to have a subject at all. Harris's *Composition No. 1*,
painted in 1940, shows how far he had travelled from *Shacks*
in 21 years.

That same year (1940), Alfred Pellan returned from
Paris and was soon producing a riot of colour and surrealist

Femme d'une pomme,
by Alfred Pellan, 1943.
Art Gallery of Ontario.

composition that was immensely influencing Canadian painting by the time Mackenzie King retired from office in 1948.
Femme d'une pomme, painted in 1943, was a far cry from the
traditional art that King and his friends had chosen for the
walls of Laurier House. •

economic sanctions to include oil, the most vital of Italy's war needs. In the midst of the international brouhaha that ensued, the King administration had to disavow its overeager representative. "Do honourable members," King asked Parliament later, "think it is Canada's role at Geneva to attempt to regulate a European war?" Few members thought it was, and Ethiopia's destruction went unmourned in Canada.

Nor was there much more sympathy for Republican Spain, threatened after 1936 by the Nationalists, led by General Francisco Franco. Franco's forces were openly Fascist, backed by the military and the Church, supported by Germany and Italy. Against this power, the legitimate Loyalist government had little success, although it too received support from abroad, notably from the Soviet Union and from its supporters throughout Europe and North America. Hundreds of Canadians, many Communist but all anti-Fascist, served the Loyalist cause in the Mackenzie-Papineau Battalion and in the largely American Lincoln and Washington Battalion. Included among their number was a Montreal doctor, Norman Bethune, who established a blood transfusion unit for the Loyalists and who, after the Spanish fight had ended in failure, went to China to assist the Communist armies there. His death in China in heroic circumstances made him a hero to hundreds of millions. In Canada he was scarcely known, and the struggles in which he had served passed without much direct attention from the Canadian government. But if the wars in Ethiopia,

King and Dr. W. A. Riddell in 1936. A barrage of headlines and a wide variety of opinions had greeted the statement by Ernest Lapointe, Acting Prime Minister, that Dr. W. A. Riddell, Canada's permanent representative at the League of Nations in 1935, was making a personal and not an official suggestion when he proposed that an oil embargo should be imposed on Mussolini's Italy. *Public Archives Canada, C-16766.*

Spain, and China seemed to suggest that Canada could remain aloof from a European crisis, few really believed it. Certainly Mackenzie King did not. He feared war and the effects it would have on Canada, but he realized that Canada would be virtually obliged to participate in a major war in which Britain became involved. English-Canadian sentiment would insist on participation and King's efforts were not directed so much at keeping Canada out of war, an impossible chore, but at encouraging the prospects of peace.

To keep peace, King believed that appeasement would work. As the major unsatisfied power, Germany had to be appeased with concessions enough that its warlike instincts would be soothed. The restrictions imposed by Versailles on German rearmament had to be relaxed and the German peoples cut off from the Reich by the peace treaties had to be brought back home. If this could be done, then Germany might just be encouraged to play a constructive role in the world. Appeasement meant settlement by negotiation, not force, and

Dr. Norman Bethune, a distinguished doctor who had served with the Loyalists in Spain and then gone to China to work with the Communist armies fighting there, died of infection and overwork in 1939. He was hailed as a hero, as this photograph of his funeral suggests, and is the most widely known Canadian in China to this day.
National Film Board, 66-3303.

King seated at his desk
in the study of Laurier
House, 1932.
*Copyright © Hands
Studios, Ottawa, Ontario;
Public Archives Canada,
C-9063.*

this course was one that attracted Mackenzie King tem-
peramentally. Of course, appeasement appealed to King
politically too. After all, what did European boundary questions mean to Canadians? The most important point was to
keep Canadians united, isolated from the quarrels of the world,
and to restore economic health to the country. Here lay the
essential reasons behind King's repudiation of Dr. Riddell's oil
sanctions. Sanctions conflicted directly with a policy of appeasement: they encouraged war, not its limitation. Far better
to negotiate than to threaten.

This Canadian position closely resembled that espoused
in Britain by Neville Chamberlain, the Prime Minister from
1937. Chamberlain also believed that Germany could be
brought to its senses by a policy of friendship and appeasement,
and his efforts in this direction shaped British policy until the
spring of 1939. But at the same time as he talked concessions,
Chamberlain was pressing British rearmament forward slowly
but surely and patching up alliances. One of his concerns, of
course, was the Commonwealth, a great reservoir of men and
supplies in the Great War. As the leading Dominion, Canada
had to be a crucial component in British planning. Where did
the great Dominion stand?

Where indeed? As early as 1934, British officials had

Ernest Lapointe.
Public Archives Canada,
C-9796.

begun to feel uneasy about Canada, finding only a "calculating aloofness" on the part of senior ministers and officials. One British visitor even felt compelled to raise what he called "the brutal question of whether Canada would come to our assistance in another war," a question that he resolved to his own satisfaction by discounting the influence of the " 'highbrows', isolationists, French Canadians, Irish disloyalists . . . and intellectuals." But the doubts lingered in Whitehall, and in 1937 the same British official told his minister, "We realize that in the present state of Canadian opinion no Canadian Government could commit itself to active participation in a war." The unsatisfactory conclusions of the Imperial Conference of 1937 reinforced this fear, for Mackenzie King once again resisted every effort by London to secure pledges in advance. The result was a British decision to plan largely around Canada: "It would be clearly disastrous if we laid our plans on the assumption that we could count on Canada, and then when the day came we found that we had been building on false promises."

To Mackenzie King, this all seemed most satisfactory. No commitments remained the keystone of his policy, for if Canada had no commitments, then the debate on foreign policy would be without focus and without danger. But curiously, just

King George VI with the prime ministers of the five dominions at the Imperial Conference of 1937.
Public Archives Canada, C-13193.

after this Imperial Conference of 1937 he visited Adolf Hitler in Berlin and told the Fuehrer that if Germany made war on Britain, Canada would be involved, a move that delighted the British, but one that appalled some isolationist and neutralist officials in the Department of External Affairs in Ottawa. That conversation with Hitler was entirely typical of King: war should be avoided by any means, but if it could not be prevented then Canada would fight.

Nevertheless, his policy of avoiding commitments continued, and constitutional experts and parliamentarians wrote endless briefs, arguing whether or not the Dominion had the right to remain neutral in the event of a British war. The legal authorities were divided, but the simple fact that Germany, for example, perceived Canada as a member of the British Commonwealth was considered certain to bring her into any war. This was the view of the British High Commissioner in Ottawa, Sir Francis Floud, who assured his superiors in London that "it is surely . . . inconceivable that Canada will not be with us in the end. All I myself really fear is a period of hesitancy . . . [that] might lengthen into perhaps two or three weeks." After all, Floud asked, "What is the alternative? Personally, I think that whatever Canada's own attitude might be, she would be brought in on our side in any case by the enemy's own action."

Of course, this speculation missed the point. King would not permit Canada to be neutral in a major British war because he knew the effects such a step would have on Canadian unity. When the Sudetenland crisis erupted in August and September 1938, for example, King's own mind was made up:

> I made it clear to both Mackenzie and Power [respectively, the Minister of National Defence and the Postmaster General] that I would stand for Canada doing all she possibly could to destroy those Powers which are basing their action on *might* and not on *right*, and that I would not consider being neutral in this situation for a moment.

Nothing could be more clear, but characteristically King said almost nothing to the public. When Chamberlain first flew off to Germany to see Hitler, King issued a statement of support for the British Prime Minister and extended his wishes for success. But neither he nor any Canadian official said what Canada's response would be if the mission to Hitler failed, although King did consider issuing a statement that "the world might as well know that should the occasion arise, Canada will not stand idly by and see modern civilization ruthlessly destroyed." The complaints of Dr. Skelton, his Under Secretary of State for External Affairs, and criticism from some cabinet ministers dissuaded the Prime Minister from issuing this pledge. Eventually, as the crisis gathered momentum, King won agreement from cabinet for a bland statement urging Canadians to stay united and adding that the government agreed with Mr. Chamberlain. But when the British, French, Italian, and German leaders met at Munich and resolved the crisis to Hitler's satisfaction by dismembering the disputed territories from Czechoslovakia, King and all Canadians were greatly relieved. The crisis had been ended through appeasement, Canada had done its part and stayed united, and matters could return to normal.

Normalcy meant making no commitments and taking no preparations. In these last few years of the 1930s, Canada was virtually defenceless. The armed forces were tiny, numbering only a few thousand men, ill-equipped, partially trained. Canada had no anti-aircraft guns, no tanks, no modern aircraft. After 1935, the King government had taken some beginning steps toward rearmament and the defence budgets gradually rose from the tiny sums ($14 million in 1932-33) allocated during the Bennett regime to $36 million in 1938-39, but it was all half-hearted. The Prime Minister's unwillingness to permit joint planning with the British military constrained policy, as did his intent to preserve Canada's no-commitments policy, an intent that extended to watching closely the kinds and types of armaments ordered for the forces.

For Mackenzie King, public opinion was important, and he moved carefully and cautiously to placate it. He knew that English Canadians would want to support Britain, a feeling that he himself shared. But he remained quite aware that opinion in Quebec was far different. Britain did not stir an emotive response there, at least not a positive one; nor did France. How could Quebec be brought along? To King it was clear: Quebec had to be assured that whatever decision Canada made about war, if it came, would be a Canadian decision alone, not one forced on the Dominion by Britain. In addition, French Can-

Their Majesties seated on the thrones in the Senate Chamber, where for the first time a reigning monarch personally gave the Royal Assent to bills passed by the Parliament of Canada.
Public Archives Canada, C-33278.

ada had to be assured that any new war would be different from the last. There would be no conscription, no massive, all-embracing war effort, no slaughter in France and Flanders.

To these ends King addressed himself during the months after the Munich crisis. On January 16, 1939, he quoted Sir Wilfrid Laurier's 1910 dictum to the House of Commons:

> If England is at war we are at war and liable to attack. I do not say that we will always be attacked; neither do I say that we would take part in all the wars of England. That is a matter that must be guided by circumstances, upon which the Canadian parliament will have to pronounce and will have to decide in its own best judgment.

That could be read soothingly everywhere in the Dominion,

Their Majesties King George VI and Queen Elizabeth at the Parliament Buildings in May 1939. Mr. King, in Windsor uniform, stands behind them.
Public Archives Canada, C-19221.

in Quebec City as well as in Toronto. Less so was King's statement on March 20, offered to the House of Commons after Hitler had violated his pledges by taking over everything that had remained of Czechoslovakia after Munich, that if the prospect of bombs falling on London came about, Canada would step forward to Britain's aid. That too forthright pledge had to be counterbalanced and ten days later King told the House of Commons that:

> The idea that every twenty years this country should automatically and as a matter of course take part in a war overseas for democracy or self-determination of other small nations, that a country which has all it can do to run itself should feel called upon to save, periodically, a continent that cannot run itself, and to these ends to risk the lives of its people, risk bankruptcy and political disunion, seems to many a nightmare and sheer madness.

That utterance was positively neutralist in tenor, but even this was balanced the next day by an activist and interventionist speech delivered by Ernest Lapointe, the Minister of Justice and King's chief colleague from Quebec.

King worried about the way he would be viewed in Canada because of his cautious speeches, afraid that he would "suffer . . . from an impression of aloofness so far as relations between Canada and Britain are concerned." But he soothed his fears by telling his diary that with Lapointe's, his speech formed "a sort of trestle sustaining the structure which would serve to unite divergent parts of Canada, thereby making for a united country." The last part of this trestle had been put into place in King's speech on March 30, when he pledged that should war come, his government would under no circumstances implement conscription for overseas service, a pledge that Bennett's successor as the leader of the Conservative Party, Dr. R. J. Manion, had independently offered one day before.

King's policy of calculated confusion had come to fruition by the spring of 1939. He had made clear that Canada would have to decide on its own about war, although he held no doubts that the decision would be for participation. To assuage Quebec's fears, he had pledged that there would be no conscription and had in effect promised a war of limited liability, a war that would not bankrupt the country or swallow up all its material or human resources. The whole effort had been geared to win time, to persuade Canadians of the rectitude of this course, and this King had largely done.

Curiously, however, the British were still mightily confused. In mid-April, after Prime Minister Chamberlain had unilaterally offered guarantees to Poland and Romania and sought an agreement with the Soviet Union without any consultation with Canada, King spoke sharply to the British High Commissioner, telling him, as the report to London went, that there was

> considerable opposition in Canada to the manner in which the United Kingdom appears to be becoming tangled with Balkan and East European countries and above all with Russia. There were many people in Canada including some ministers, and I gathered this included [King], who disliked entanglements of this kind. . . . He could not forecast in advance of Parliament what line Canada would take if the United Kingdom went to the help of one of these countries and as a result were herself attacked.

British policy was foolish, Mackenzie King believed, for with these guarantees Chamberlain had abandoned appeasement, a policy that in King's view had not yet failed, and the Canadian took out his resentment on the hapless High Commissioner. Ironically, the very same day, April 24, King and Dr. Skelton agreed that "Germany knew quite well that Canada would go into the fight if Germany were in any way an aggressor."

The Prime Minister, therefore, had prepared himself for war, if and when it came. The final public opinion preparations were made in May and June 1939 when King George VI and Queen Elizabeth came to Canada for a long Royal Tour. The crowds were ecstatic everywhere and pro-British sentiment was at its peak. The visit had been planned to solidify Canada behind the Empire and it did its work well. The biographer of George VI, J. W. Wheeler-Bennett, noted approvingly that neutrality sentiment in Canada disappeared after the visit "like thin clouds before a Biscay gale."

The final and inevitable crisis came in August 1939 when Hitler stepped up his pressure on the Poles. Canada was not directly consulted by Britain as it manoeuvered feverishly in the last few days of peace, exactly as Canada had not been consulted before Britain gave its guarantee to the Poles. On August 25, a discouraged and frustrated Dr. Skelton wrote to Mackenzie King that

The first casualty of this war has been Canada's claim to control over her own destinies. If war comes to Poland and we take part, that war came as a consequence of commitments made by the Government of Great Britain, about which we were not given the slightest inkling of information in advance.

That was true enough, but Mackenzie King had never sought to be consulted about British policy. His preferred course had been followed by the British who had told him after the fact about their policy decisions. Unfortunately, the events of the late 1930s did directly involve Canada and Canadians in the threat of war, and on such questions something more than after-the-fact participation was required. Still, in King's judgment — and his judgment was usually good and careful — the risks to national unity would have been too great if Canada had debated the issues fully and frankly. It was far better that Canada should go to war for Britain than that it should go for itself. That is what happened in September 1939.

6
At War

THE GERMAN ARMIES invaded Poland early in the morning
of September 1, 1939, and almost instantly began racing well
ahead of their schedules. For the Western powers the invasion,
while not unexpected, posed serious problems. They could not
get aid to the Poles in time for it to be of any use; besides, no
one contemplated a major offensive in the West, a diversionary
tactic that might have drawn enough German troops away to
defend the Fatherland so that Poland could defend itself better.
Worse, in the British Prime Minister's residence at 10 Downing
Street, Neville Chamberlain made a feverish effort to shirk the
commitments made to Poland six months earlier, an effort that
was balked only by threatened resignations in cabinet. After
agonizing over the decision for 48 hours, Britain issued its
declaration of war on September 3. France also declared war
on Germany. World War II had begun.

For Canada and Mackenzie King, everything went as
planned. At a cabinet meeting on August 24, as the final crisis
broke, the Prime Minister secured the agreement of his colleagues that "in the event of war we had now decided that
Canada would participate . . . that we would summon Parliament at the moment war was declared." On September 3,
Parliament was called to meet four days later. For the moment
Canada was still technically neutral, although Ian Mackenzie,
the Minister of National Defence, told his officers "that they
were to give effect to all the defence measures which would be
required in a state of war and to fire on any blinking German
who came within range of our guns — but that we were not
at war."

Few guns could have hit anyone. The military chiefs
had prepared a plan for submission to the Cabinet on August
30 that envisaged an army of 60,000 to be readied for despatch
overseas as soon as possible. This proposal shocked King, who
believed that it flew in the face of his oft-repeated pledges that

Parliament would decide if Canada was at war and what form the Canadian contribution would take, and he shortly issued orders that expenditures except for the defence of Canada would be refused approval. Mackenzie King's position, however short-sighted it may seem in retrospect, was not taken simply because it conformed with his prejudices and predilections. He had learned from the British High Commissioner and from Prime Minister Chamberlain that London saw Canada's primary role as "the defence of Canada," an implicit acceptance of the idea that an expeditionary force was not required.

This was the position when Parliament met in Ottawa in emergency special session on September 7. The Speech from the Throne informed the assembled Senators and Members that they had been summoned "in order that the government

The first Canadian troops to go overseas in World War II embarking at Halifax in December 1939. *Public Archives Canada, C-14458.*

War loan posters.
Public Archives Canada,
C-33446 and C-5787.

may seek authority for the measures necessary for the defence of Canada and for co-operation in the determined effort which is being made to resist further aggression." The next day, Mackenzie King delivered his initial major address, the first real statement of his government's policy:

> We stand for the defence of Canada; we stand for co-operation of this country at the side of Great Britain; and if this house will not support us in that policy, it will have to find some other government to assume the responsibilities of the present.

That was clear and straightforward. King then explained the reasons for his tortuous course in external policy since his return to office in 1935:

> I have never doubted that when the fatal moment came, the free spirit of the Canadian people would assert itself in the preservation and defence of freedom. . . . I have, however, been anxious that when the inevitable hour came, our people should be as one from coast to coast in recognizing the magnitude of the issue which was presenting itself, and as

The War Committee of the cabinet in 1943. Front row, left to right: Hon. C. G. Power, Minister of National Defence for Air; Hon. T. A. Crerar, Minister of Mines and Resources; the Prime Minister; Hon. J. L. Ralston, Minister of National Defence; Hon. J. L. Ilsley, Minister of Finance. Back row: Hon. A. L. Macdonald, Minister of National Defence for Naval Services; Hon. J. E. Michaud, Minister of Transport; Hon. C. D. Howe, Minister of Munitions and Supply, and Hon. Louis S. St. Laurent, Minister of Justice. *Public Archives Canada, C-26922.*

one in their determination to meet it with all the strength and power at their command. I have made it, therefore, the supreme endeavour of my leadership of my party, and my leadership of the government of this country, to let no hasty or premature threat or pronouncement create mistrust and divisions between the different elements that compose the population of our vast dominion, so that when the moment of decision came all should so see the issue itself that our national effort might be marked by unity of purpose, of heart and of endeavour.

His policy had been to bring a united Canada into the war, King said, and to ensure this he repeated his pledge of March 30, 1939: "The present government believe that conscription of men for overseas service will not be a necessary or effective step. No such measure will be introduced by the present administration." No pledge could have been more unequivocal.

King's policy received its vindication when Parliament approved without division the Address in Reply to the Speech from the Throne, a vote that King had indicated would denote support for a declaration of war. A few Quebec isolationist members spoke against participation, a few reflective of a much larger number in their province, but the highlight of the session was a moving address by the CCF leader, J. S. Woodsworth, a convinced pacifist:

I do not care whether you think me an impossible idealist or a dangerous crank, I am going to take my place beside the children and these young people, because it is only as we adopt new policies that this world will be at all a livable place.... We laud the courage of those who go to the front; yes, I have boys of my own, and I hope they are not cowards, but if any one of those boys, not from cowardice but really through belief, is willing to take his stand on this matter ... I shall be more proud of that boy than if he enlisted for the war.

Woodsworth's pacifism, of course, was a minority view in the country, but he expressed thoughts that had to be voiced, thoughts that did Canada, Parliament, and Woodsworth himself credit.

So Canada was at war. King George VI signed the declaration on September 10, and when Mackenzie King received word that a state of war now existed between Canada and Germany, "I knelt and prayed for my country and for the cause of freedom, for strength and guidance in these times of need." But what was the war about? Was it a war for freedom and democracy? a war for Poland? a war to avenge the persecuted Jews? even a war against Nazism? Hardly. The war began with German aggression, but Britain was involved only because of pledges made hastily by Chamberlain, pledges

Mackenzie King and Winston Churchill in London in August 1941. This was their first meeting during World War II. King noted in his diary that in spite of the cares of war, Churchill "looked as fresh as could be, and really more youthful than I have seen him on different occasions." Both were the same age — 67. *Public Archives Canada, C-47565.*

An informal photograph of General A. G. L. McNaughton, taken in England during the winter of 1939-40, when he was commander of the First Canadian Division. *Public Archives Canada, PA-34159.*

that the British Prime Minister had tried to avoid honouring. For Canada, it was even less clear. Canada had not played a role of any consequence in the pre-war manoeuvering, and it went to war for one reason alone: because Britain went to war. No one made hard-headed assessments of Canadian national interests or potential consequences. Canada went to war on September 10, 1939 much as it had gone a quarter-century before. All that differed was the separate declaration of war, a small reward for 25 years of advance to autonomy. Eventually the war would become a genuine crusade for freedom, a truly just war against evil, but it would take defeats, bloodshed, and the revelation of unspeakable horrors in concentration camps before people came to this view.

Certainly there was little enthusiasm for the war in Canada to begin with. It was a duty, an unpleasant duty that had to be met, but there was no enthusiasm anywhere, particularly not in Quebec. On the other hand, there were no demonstrations against the war in the French-speaking province, primarily because King had played his hand so well, and because the prime ministerial pledges against conscription were believed. Still, two weeks after the Canadian declaration, Premier Duplessis called a snap election ostensibly on the issue that Ottawa was using the war to increase centralization and destroy provincial autonomy. In fact, the issue was the war, and this Union Nationale challenge threatened to shatter the fragile consensus King had created. Against his wishes, the

Quebec ministers in the federal cabinet, Ernest Lapointe, C. G. Power and P. J. A. Cardin, entered the election campaign directly. In speech after speech, Lapointe attacked Duplessis and urged his defeat. King had promised no conscription, Lapointe said, and he reaffirmed this pledge. If Quebec returned the Union Nationale this would be a vote against the province's representatives in the cabinet in Ottawa, and he, Cardin, and Power would resign their posts, leaving only an English-speaking cabinet. That threat, implying that the barriers to a conscriptionist government would be down, apparently shook the voters, and on October 25, Duplessis suffered a crushing defeat at the hands of Adelard Godbout, the Quebec Liberal leader. The victory, however, belonged to Lapointe. The first attack on Ottawa's policies had been met.

Meanwhile, the government had determined to despatch an expeditionary force of one division to Britain and given command of it to General A. G. L. McNaughton, a distinguished artillery commander in the Great War and a scientist of note who seemed likely to be as cautious of his men's lives as possible. There was some heart-searching before

The raid that failed: a German photograph of Canadian dead and shattered equipment on the beach at Dieppe on the day of the attempted landing on August 19, 1942. *Public Archives Canada, C-14160.*

the decision to send troops abroad was taken, but King felt he had no option — the moderate patriotic ardour of English Canada had to be served. A few days later, the cabinet learned of a British proposal for a great Commonwealth air training scheme, a plan that would use Canada as its main training ground. This was a more congenial proposal to Mackenzie King, for air war seemed less likely to produce casualties than trench warfare on Great War lines, and casualties held out the horrific prospect of reinforcement shortages and a struggle for conscription. As a result, the Canadian ministers were enthusiastic, until they learned that Britain expected Canada to pay more than half of the cost of the scheme — an estimated $375 million out of a total of $600 million. This sum staggered the cabinet. The total national budget before the war had been only $600 million and the war expenditures approved by Parliament amounted to an extra $100 million. The Depression still hung over the land, so where could Canada find the money?

The negotiations between the British air mission and the cabinet were long and hard and the name-calling became sharp at times. The Australians and New Zealanders, also involved in the program, carefully watched the costs too, while the wires

Hon. C. D. Howe, Minister of Munitions and Supply, receiving a 25-pound shell from Ms. Edna Poirier. Canadian munitions workers, many of whom were women, turned out hundreds of *millions* of these and other weapons.
Public Archives Canada, C-7487.

"GO ON, SPEND IT...
what's the difference?"

CANADIANS . . . the time has come when every nickel, dime and quarter you spend *needlessly* is money spent in the cause of our enemies! NOW, more than any time since this war began, national THRIFT is essential.

And THRIFT begins with those little things you *needlessly* buy from day to day—THRIFT begins in the home, in the kitchen, in the clothes you wear. From now on, resolve that *needless* spending is out! *Your* personal war job is to save every cent you can . . . and invest those savings in War Savings Stamps!

Yes, saving to buy War Savings Stamps is a *vital* war job for every woman, man and child in Canada. War saving stamps are a protection NOW and an investment for the future which will bring you back $5 for every $4 you invest.

So remember—let THRIFT be your watchword! Every day, save a little—and invest those savings in War Savings Stamps.

Buy War Savings Stamps from banks, post offices, druggists, grocers and other retail stores—and buy them regularly.

Buy WAR SAVINGS STAMPS EVERY WEEK

SAVING IS SERVING

NATIONAL WAR FINANCE COMMITTEE

hummed between Ottawa and London. In the end, the total cost of the scheme was fixed at $607 million, of which Britain would pay $185 million, Australia $39.9 million, New Zealand $28 million, while the lion's share of $353.4 million was to be paid by Canada. Delighted that the final agreement was signed on his birthday, December 17, King consoled himself about the huge Canadian share of the cost by noting that the heavy expenses would not come at the beginning of the plan and "if war lasts two years or more, people . . . will be ready to stand the higher outlays." The British Commonwealth Air Training Plan, as it came to be known, became unquestionably the most important Canadian military contribution to the war, producing thousands and thousands of pilots, observers, air gunners, and navigators for the great air fleets that levelled Germany. It also served the more immediate purpose of being a great help to Mackenzie King in winning the election of 1940.

That election burst unexpectedly on the country — and on Mackenzie King. The Prime Minister had been contemplating a general election for some time, but he had postponed all thoughts of it with the advent of the Polish crisis in the summer of 1939; he had even promised Dr. Manion, the Tory leader, that Parliament would meet for a full session in 1940 before dissolution. That was his genuine intent — at that

Ground crew servicing a Catalina flying boat of No. 413 (Coastal) Squadron, RCAF, in Ceylon, August 1942. This squadron spent two and a half years operating over the Indian Ocean as part of the South-East Asia Air Command.
Public Archives Canada, PL-10008.

time. But early in January 1940, Premier Mitchell Hepburn attacked Ottawa's war effort in the Ontario Legislature and gave King the idea that he could move quickly and nip his opposition in the bud.

At Queen's Park, Hepburn, seething about the slow rate of Canadian war preparations, impulsively moved a resolution deploring "that the Federal Government at Ottawa had made so little effort to prosecute Canada's duty in the war in the vigorous manner the people of Canada desire to see." This resolution, cheerfully agreed to by George Drew, the leader of the Conservative party at Queen's Park, easily passed. It gave Mackenzie King a heaven-sent opportunity:

> Hepburn's action has given to me and my colleagues and to the party here just what is needed to place beyond question the wisdom of an immediate election and the assurance of victory for the Government. What really has helped to take an enormous load off my mind is that it justified an immediate appeal, avoiding thereby all the contention of a session known to be immediately preceding an election.

Moreover, King added, the greatest relief of all "is the probability of having the election over before the worst of the fighting begins in Europe." That was prescience indeed: "I have dreaded having to choose the moment for the campaign and specially to choose it at a time when human lives are being slaughtered by hundreds of thousands, if not by millions."

A few days later on January 25, 1940, and following conditions of the utmost secrecy, the Governor General read the Speech from the Throne to the parliamentarians assembled for the opening of the 1940 session. In a stunned hush, the Members heard His Excellency announce an immediate dissolution. Only with difficulty did Dr. Manion and J. S. Woodsworth even get the floor to voice a few complaints, Manion in particular raging because of what he considered King's going back on his pledged word. "Nothing," King wrote, "hurts me more than when the situation becomes personal and one's own position becomes misrepresented. That, of course, is the hardest cross to be borne in public life."

King's snap dissolution caught the Opposition unprepared. But the next day, the Conservatives met in caucus and, somewhat inexplicably, decided to campaign on the issue of national government, a government of the "best brains in the country." This issue, smacking as it did of Union Government in 1917, was the worst the Tories could have picked. It persuaded Quebec instantly that the Tories wanted conscription again, and it seems to have led English Canadians to the view that Manion wanted a massive war effort on the scale of the Great War. Few in Canada desired either conscription or total war in January 1940, and the national government issue became a heavy albatross around Manion's neck. Again and again he repeated that he was opposed to conscription; but again and again editorial writers and critics pointed to his autobiography, *Life is an Adventure*, published in 1936, where he had affirmed a belief in compulsory military service.

For Mackenzie King and the Liberals the situation was ideal. Manion and the National Government were suspect because people feared they would do too much. The CCF was suspect because it was too lukewarm on the war. Only the Liberals held the middle ground of a moderate war effort without conscription, a position that party strategists had carved out. One key campaign memorandum observed realistically and cynically that Liberals should "blow both hot and cold on the

Prime Minister Churchill, President Roosevelt, and Mr. King at a press conference in the Citadel at Quebec at the conclusion of the second Quebec Conference in September 1944.
Public Archives Canada, C-26932.

subject of preparedness for war," assuming "that only in the Province of Ontario does Canada's wartime effort almost completely overshadow all considerations of the normal functions of Government and the peacetime concerns of the people." Elsewhere, the memorandum on strategy continued, "We assume that the war effort is of primary importance but that public opinion is also interested in the Government's peacetime measures and general policies." A very shrewd and cool assessment and one that shaped the King campaign.

The campaign went according to plan. Manion huffed and puffed under constant attack from the press for his abusive language and under pressure from some elements in his party who wanted conscription and other groups that feared Manion was too radical on social questions. King, buoyantly predicting a sweep, did a national tour and made several radio addresses. His party was flush with campaign funds and running far ahead of the opposition. It was a cakewalk, and the government was returned on March 26 with 181 seats, the largest majority ever. Manion was defeated in his constituency and the Tories elected only 40 members, the CCF eight, and Social Credit 10. Even more impressive, the Liberals won 51.5 per cent of the national popular vote, an astonishing feat in a four-party election, a tribute to King's stewardship and to the public's desire not to change horses in midstream.

King's good fortune in having the election out of the way before the campaigning season began in Europe soon became apparent. In April, the Nazis invaded Denmark and Norway and the following month the full weight of the *Wehrmacht* fell on the Low Countries and France. With stunning speed, the Allied positions in Belgium and France collapsed, and the retreat turned into a rout, only partially redeemed by the fortuitous evacuation at Dunkirk. For the single Canadian division, in Britain since December 1939, the Fall of France verged on tragic farce. The Canadian Division was despatched to France early in June, disembarked from its troopships, and sent by rail into the interior. At this point, the recall came and the division reboarded its ships and departed for England — leaving much of its heavy equipment behind. With their return to England, the Canadians became almost the only trained and relatively well-equipped division standing in the way of a German invasion of Britain.

At home the shock of the defeats fell with tremendous force. From being a subsidiary ally fighting a limited-liability war, Canada suddenly was the ranking ally of Britain, fighting desperately for its life. The financial limitations on the war effort were jettisoned, and Canada — like Britain — began to take the war seriously.

The first major effect of this new situation was the passage of the National Resources Mobilization Act a few days after the French capitulation in mid-June. The NRMA gave King's government sweeping powers to control industry and manpower, but its major purpose was to launch a scheme of home defence conscription. Men would be called up, initially, for 30 days training (a period that the government eventually lengthened to three months and then to the duration of the war). King had never pledged himself against conscription for the defence of Canada, only for overseas service, and the NRMA met with remarkably little criticism anywhere. In Quebec, the people accepted the idea that compulsion for the defence of the homeland was necessary, and the one major incident — the arrest and incarceration of the Mayor of Montreal, Camillien Houde, for urging his compatriots not to register in the government's great National Registration of August 1940 — passed off with scarcely a murmur. Soon young men were called up for service, for thirty days of rudimentary military training, sports, and clean living designed to end what one officer called "twenty years of pacifist debauchery."

At the same time, recruits flocked to the colours. By the end of 1939 the army had enlisted 65,000 men, but in June, July, and August 1940, the numbers volunteering for service anywhere numbered 29,319, 29,171, and 15,934 respectively. Air force and navy enlistments rose similarly. A second infantry division joined the 1939 arrivals in Britain; on Christmas Day 1940 a Canadian Corps, the direct successor of the famous Canadian formation of the Great War, was created under General McNaughton's command.

War production began to boom as well. In the first months of the war, it had been sluggish, partly because of the Canadian financial constraints but also because British orders were tiny and slow to arrive. The British had their own unemployment at home to concern them, and the United Kingdom government reacted predictably to pressures from domestic industries by giving the orders to Sheffield, Birmingham, and Coventry. The result was that, by the beginning of June 1940, only $90 million in British orders had been placed in Canada, a matter that infuriated Mackenzie King. In a telegram to Winston Churchill, England's Prime Minister since May 10, King was blunt:

. . . I must express to you the sincere regret that is felt not less by the Canadian people than by my colleagues and myself that the resources and industry of Canada are not being afforded an opportunity to make anything like their full contribution to Britain's war programme, and that the authorities responsible for British purchases have not recognized the potential capacity of our industry to produce munitions.

Those representations had the desired effect and the British purchasing organization and procedures altered quickly. Thereafter Britain would take virtually everything Canada could give without much worry over the price of specific items.

The result was extraordinary growth in war production, marshalled and directed by C. D. Howe, the Minister of Munitions and Supply. In 1939 and 1940 all told, production was only $310 million for war purposes, but the next year it rose to $810 million, and in 1942, in an astonishing increase, it reached $2,060,000,000. From there it continued to increase each year. Most of this production was for Great Britain, and all too soon the war material came forth in quantities that exceeded the British ability to pay. Inevitably Canada found itself in some financial difficulties as a result, so various measures had to be taken to keep production going while not bankrupting the nation. One expedient was the repatriation of hundreds of millions of dollars of bonds and debentures held in Britain by British investors in Canadian government and industrial issues. Another expedient was a large low-interest loan. Yet a third was a gift of $1 billion to Britain at the beginning of 1942, a massive gesture almost double the pre-war national budget. This present was followed in 1943 by the Mutual Aid Act which allocated a further $1 billion for assistance to the Allies and huge supplemental sums were added the next year and the year following. In all, by the war's end Britain had received $3,468,000,000 in gifts from Canada and more in loans.

This unparalleled generosity — it far exceeded *per capita* the similar American Lend-Lease programs — was made possible only by the growth in the economy under the impact of the war. The Minister of Finance, J. L. Ilsley, guided the economy as federal government revenues mounted extraordinarily, reaching more than $2.4 billion in 1943-44 as new taxes and duties poured money into the treasury at a rate almost six times higher than before the war. But expenditures far exceeded revenues and in that same fiscal year the government spent $5,322,000,000, an amount that increased the national debt. The limited-liability war in the financial sphere was gone, as every income-tax payer could testify. For example, take the case of a married man with two children:

Taxes

Income	Pre-war	1939	1940	1941	1943
$ 1500	—	—	$ 14	$ 35	$ 24 + $ 24*
$ 3000	$ 9	$ 10	$ 97	$ 215	$ 334 + $ 334*
$ 5000	$118	$134	$ 427	$ 735	$1062 + $ 600*
$10,000	$660	$738	$1921	$2710	$3346 + $1200*

*This additional amount represents the money Canadian taxpayers were obliged to save.

Everyone paid for the war, and millions more were contributed in Victory Bonds, in war savings stamps sold to school children, and in contributions to patriotic organizations.

The great difficulty for the government, giving millions in goods without payment to Britain, was to regularize its situation with the United States. Fortunately Mackenzie King and President Franklin D. Roosevelt had developed since 1935 a genuinely cordial relationship that would be the financial and military salvation of Canada. In 1935 and 1938, trade agreements had been signed between the two countries and, as the cloud of war drew closer, Roosevelt pledged that the United States would assist Canada in defending itself. In August 1940, after the debacle in France, King and Roosevelt met at Ogdensburg, New York, to draft a joint statement that tied the defences of the two North American states closely together for the first time. A Permanent Joint Board on Defence was created with representatives from both countries with the power to advise on defence measures. In war economics, the links were also close. Both countries faced similar problems because much of their overseas trade was cut off by German conquests, and both had to share scarce continental resources. But the Canadian problem was that this country's balance of trade deficit with the Americans had increased rapidly, thanks to the necessity to purchase more goods in the United States for conversion into war supplies for Britain. Before the war Canada had had a surplus in trade with Britain that balanced the perpetual deficit with the U.S., but now Britain could no longer pay. The solution, cemented

OPPOSITE *The Competitor*, by R. Tait McKenzie. *The National Gallery of Canada, Ottawa.*

by King and Roosevelt in the Hyde Park Declaration in April 1941, was for the United States to give Canada the components of war material intended for Britain under Lend-Lease on the British account, thus relieving Canada of the necessity of spending scarce American dollars for them. In addition, the Americans agreed to increase their purchases in Canada of resource materials. The effect was to ease the balance of payments crisis and to permit Canada to continue financing the war without destroying its credit or ruining its economy.

The strains on the economy continued to increase nonetheless. The war had begun an inflationary spiral, something that in its early days was not unwelcome after the deflation of the Depression. But that spiral continued to mount, and in the spring of 1941 it began to accelerate. In seven months the cost of living index rose some five per cent, more than in the entire year before. The government's response was bold and direct. In a broadcast to the country on October 18, 1941, Mackenzie King announced a sweeping program of wage and price controls. "It will affect the daily lives of each one of us," the Prime Minister said. "It will require the cooperation and support of all. It will help to intensify the effort of this country in war. It will help to prevent a repetition of distress and depression after the war." After December 1, 1941, King ordered, "No person may sell any goods or supply any services at a price or rate higher than that charged by him for such goods and services during the four weeks from September 15 to October 11. . . . Except in cases where minimum prices are fixed, prices will be free to fall below the ceiling." The freeze was total, and it would be administered by the Wartime Prices and Trade Board, headed by a civil servant of remarkable dynamism and integrity, Donald Gordon. The wPTB's efforts ended inflation in Canada for the duration of the war and the cost of living stayed fixed. In fact, some prices actually fell between October 1941 and the end of the war. The overall record of controls in Canada was the best of any belligerent nation — on the Allied or the Axis side.

The wPTB also had charge of rationing scarce goods in Canada. Sugar, tea, coffee, butter, and gasoline were all rationed in 1942, and the next year meat was added to the list. Consumers began to save fats, count their coupons, and hoard their blue meat discs, while tires and gas became scarce commodities for all but essential users. In fact, however, the rationing was never very severe, so rich had the nation become and so productive its agriculture during the war. The low point for butter rations, for example, was six ounces per person per week; meat rations varied from one to two-and-a-half pounds per person per week depending on cut; even imported coffee never dropped below four ounces per person per week. The war on the home front was hard some of the time, but it was never stringent, except for taxation.

Abroad, the war was stringent indeed; worse, it was going very badly for the Allies. The initial German successes in 1940 were followed by speedy conquests in Greece and Yugoslavia and joint German-Italian advances in North Africa. On June 22, 1941, the Germans launched history's greatest land assault and attacked the Soviet Union along a 1500 mile front, swiftly cutting deep into Russia. The war was in danger of being lost, the sole bright spot being the defeat of German airpower in the Battle of Britain in the fall of 1940. Then in the midst of further initial defeats, the tide turned. On December 7, 1941, the Japanese attacked Pearl Harbor in the Hawaiian Islands and a number of additional British and American bases in the Pacific. Everywhere the Japanese met success, but by at last bringing the great industrial and military power of the United States into the war, they guaranteed eventual Allied success.

The losses were heavy, however. For Canada, the Japanese assault at Hong Kong was especially severe, for some 2000 Canadian soldiers had been stationed there in response to a British request made a few months before. The troops were adequately trained, but they had not yet become acclimatized to the rough Hong Kong terrain when they found themselves facing overwhelming numbers in a fight for their lives. The battle lasted little more than two weeks, the remnants of the hungry and thirsty garrison surrendering the Crown colony on Christmas Day 1941. Every one of the Canadians was killed or captured; the dead became the envy of the living as the horrors and cruelties of Japanese prison camp captivity became apparent.

This first test of Canadian arms had not been successful; nor was the next. Dieppe is a small coastal town in France and in 1942 the Allied commanders selected it as the locale for a test of invasion techniques. Could a fortified port be taken from the sea? That was the question the 2nd Canadian Division set out to answer on August 19, 1942. From England, 4963 Canadians embarked on the operation and only 2210 returned. Despite hard fighting and individual acts of great gallantry, the Dieppe raid turned into a disaster, for the Germans, alert and

The greater raid that succeeded: Canadian infantry streaming ashore at Bernières-sur-Mer, on the Normandy Coast, on D-Day, June 6, 1944. *Copyright © Whitcombe, Gilmour & Company, Montreal; Public Archives Canada, C-14765.*

prepared, simply cut down the troops and disabled their tanks on the beaches. Some men reached their objectives inland, but nothing mattered in the face of the heavy casualties. The Royal Regiment of Canada, a Toronto battalion, suffered 209 killed, the heaviest toll sustained by a single Canadian unit in one day in the war. It was a slaughter; the long casualty lists in the newspapers brought home to Canadians that the war would not be won without its payment in blood.

At sea there was blood too. The tiny Canadian Navy expanded rapidly from the outbreak of war and fought its way through the Battle of the Atlantic. The German U-boat was the enemy and the shepherding of convoys across the sea to Britain the task. By 1943, the RCN was providing 48 per cent of the North Atlantic convoy escort, and Canadian senior officers held command of the vital northwest Atlantic sector. It was a far cry from the days of a two-ship navy virtually without funds.

Canadians also served with great gallantry and in large numbers in the air. The British Commonwealth Air Training

Plan eventually produced some 82,000 trained aircrew who went overseas to fly against the Germans or the Japanese. More than 40 Royal Canadian Air Force squadrons, flying fighters, bombers, transports, and other aircraft were stationed in Britain. Thousands more RCAF men served in units of the Royal Air Force, a sore point to many in Canada, including the Minister of National Defence for Air, Chubby Power, who fought for the right for Canadians to be concentrated in Canadian units commanded by Canadian officers. The bombers suffered particularly heavy losses in their raids on the heavily fortified German targets; between March and July 1943, for example, No. 6 Group, a 13-squadron Canadian bomber group, lost 638 aircrew and 118 aircraft. About five per cent of the aircraft never returned to bases in England. The air war was a terribly costly one, especially for the German civilians who paid for the folly and criminal greed of their Fuehrer.

After Dieppe, the next major Canadian battle on land came in Sicily in July 1943, where the 1st Canadian Division under General Guy Simonds, perhaps the best Canadian general officer of the war, participated in the invasion and subsequent short but sharp campaign that successfully drove the Germans off the island. The Canadians stayed in the Mediterranean for the invasion of Italy and, expanded to a corps, fought their way up the Italian boot in difficult conditions. At Ortona in December 1943, troopers from the Loyal Edmonton Regiment, the Seaforth Highlanders, and the Three Rivers Regiment, a good cross-section of Canadians from all across the country, fought and defeated crack German paratroops, a battle punctuated by staggered two-hour respites for Christmas dinners as companies were pulled out of the line in turn.

The climax of the war on land came in North West Europe, and began with the invasion of Normandy on D-Day, June 6, 1944. The 3rd Canadian Division took part in the assault, met its objectives, and acquitted itself brilliantly. Soon it was joined by additional troops until the First Canadian Army, the largest formation ever commanded and staffed by Canadians, was in the field. The Canadian task was largely to hold the sea flank of the Anglo-American-Canadian front in France and the Low Countries, a chore that involved the Canadians in very severe fighting in the Scheldt estuary. Casualties were heavy, particularly to the infantry, as the Germans continued to resist all the more fiercely the closer the war drew to Germany. Between October 1, 1944, and November 8, 1944, for example, the Canadians suffered 6367 casualties in clearing the Scheldt and opening the port of Antwerp to Allied shipping.

Those casualties and the thousands that preceded and followed them precipitated the greatest political crisis of the war in Canada. The conscription crisis of 1944 very nearly destroyed the government of Mackenzie King and could conceivably have produced something akin to civil war in Canada. That it did not do either shows Mackenzie King's political skill, ruthlessness, and sagacity.

The crisis had been a long time in gestation. The recruiting of men for overseas service had proceeded well through the spring of 1941 with no difficulties in filling quotas. In May of that year, the first organized recruiting campaign had been launched, and it exceeded its requirements in volunteers. But some in the country were convinced that conscription was the only way to fight a total war; indeed, to them conscription was the sign of a total war. One such advocate of conscription was Arthur Meighen, the old Conservative leader defeated by King in the 1920s. A Senator since 1932, Meighen remained the same man he had always been, intelligent, hardnosed, and convinced that King's way had to be the wrong way. To Meighen, overseas conscription had to come. What, he asked, was the point of conscripting men to defend Canada when the war had to be won overseas? In November 1941 Meighen became leader of his party once more after a regular party meeting had been converted into a leadership quasi-convention, and his selection was whooped through. As his policy, Meighen proclaimed conscription and national government, the policy of 1917 all over again.

The threat of Meighen shook the King government. The Prime Minister feared his venomous tongue and feared what he and conscription could do to public opinion. But many inside the cabinet worried about the personnel situation, too, most notably Colonel J. Layton Ralston, the Minister of National Defence. Ralston had been a courageous and able battalion commander in the Great War, and he was a great rock of a man concerned about the welfare of the boys overseas. He knew reinforcements were plentiful at the end of 1941 — how could there be a shortage when there had been few casualties as yet? — but he feared that there might be problems when casualties began to mount. To Ralston, the government needed the power to conscript men now so that it could be prepared for the worst. In this view he was joined

by, among others, Angus Macdonald, the Minister of National Defence for Naval Services and the former Premier of Nova Scotia.

King could not agree. He had promised that there would be no conscription, and he had won his election on this pledge in 1940. Could he go back on his word now at a time when casualties were low? It was not that King was emotionally an anti-conscriptionist, not at all. He was and remained a pragmatist; as such, he could see the effect conscription would have on Quebec. French Canadians shared in this war far more than in the last, and the number of men in Quebec enlisting for service was far greater, too. Would all these gains be lost if he moved for conscription? But Meighen outside the cabinet and Ralston inside were calling for conscription: King was torn. Then in a brilliant flash of inspiration he found his solution: he would ask the people in a plebiscite to release the government from its pledges about the methods of raising men. That would settle down Ralston and it would cut Meighen's conscription campaign off at the knees, for people would vote in the plebiscite on the question and not have to engage in a destructive guerrilla war against the government. A plebiscite would also have the useful purpose of hurting Meighen's campaign in the Toronto riding of York South where he was fighting to win a seat in the House of Commons in a by-election. This last purpose, at least, was quickly accomplished when Meighen fell before the effective welfare-oriented campaign of an unknown CCF candidate, high-school teacher Joseph Noseworthy, in a riding that had hitherto always been Tory. The leader of the Conservatives had been finally disposed of; now Quebec remained to be persuaded.

This would not be so easy, thanks to a remarkable pressure group, *La Ligue pour la défense du Canada*, that was organized by a number of *nationaliste* organizations to fight the plebiscite. The *Ligue*'s position was simple: King and Lapointe had promised no conscription to Quebec in 1939 and 1940. Now King was asking all Canada to repudiate a pledge made to Quebec, a violation of the bargain. Moreover, once the government got its "Yes" vote on the plebiscite, conscription would surely be implemented. Quebec was prepared to defend Canada, *Ligue* spokespersons said, but French Canadians would never accept conscription for service abroad. This message was carried to every home in the province in a campaign funded with nickels, dimes, and dollar bills and staffed by thousands of volunteers. The press and the radio were largely shut off to the *Ligue*, but the message got through nonetheless, and in the plebiscite at the end of April 1942 Quebec voted "*Non*," 72.9 per cent of its electors supporting the *Ligue*'s position. In the rest of the provinces heavy majorities endorsed the government's appeal, leaving Mackenzie King faced with another dilemma.

What could he do now? If he didn't move on conscription he might lose Ralston and Macdonald (and Ralston at one point submitted his resignation only to hold it in abeyance); if he did take action he stood to lose the Quebec ministers and to alienate irrevocably the province of Quebec. His solution was masterful and one reached after agonizing appraisals of his situation. He would move to amend the National Resources Mobilization Act by deleting from it the clause that limited conscription to home service, but as he told Parliament in a

King talking to aircrew of No. 425 (Alouette) Squadron, RCAF at Tholthorpe, Yorkshire, in May 1944.
Public Archives Canada, PL-29604.

Members of the Women's Royal Canadian Naval Service (known, like their Royal Navy sisters, as the "Wrens") on board HMCS *Sudbury* at Halifax in 1943.
Public Archives Canada, GM-539.

brilliant phrase that immediately became part of our folklore, his policy was "not necessarily conscription, but conscription if necessary." That expressed it neatly: the government would have the power to conscript for overseas service, but that power would not be exercised unless it became absolutely necessary to do so. One French-speaking minister, P. J. A. Cardin, left the cabinet in protest, but the remainder stayed firm. Ernest Lapointe had died the November before and his replacement as King's Quebec lieutenant, Louis St. Laurent, a Quebec City lawyer, brought new strength to the government and a calm head — he stayed too.

King's delaying effectively stilled the conscription controversy for more than two years. Recruiting kept up and, although casualties were heavy at Dieppe, in Sicily, and in Italy, the reinforcement system worked well. There were no major problems until D-Day and the Normandy invasion put the entire Canadian Army into battle. Then casualties began to soar, particularly among front-line infantry, something that Allied planners and staff officers had underestimated. At no time would the Canadian Army suffer from an overall shortage of reinforcements, but it would have a shortage of infantry.

The crisis blew up in October 1944 when Colonel Ralston

returned from a visit to the front. The Minister believed that the Army overseas faced a shortage of reinforcements in the months ahead that could be met only by taking men from the home-defence conscripts still serving in Canada. The NRMA had approximately 60,000 soldiers, many of whom had been training in Canada since 1941. These men had resisted efforts to persuade them to volunteer for overseas service, and it seemed unlikely that they would willingly go overseas unless they were conscripted. Now Ralston believed the time had come.

The cabinet was completely unprepared for the shock of Ralston's advice — every word from the front had said that reinforcements were in good supply. Moreover, by the end of 1944 it was clear that Germany could not last long. The Russian steamroller pressed ever westward while the Allies moved east, and Hitler's Reich became squeezed in a vise. Mackenzie King, in particular, was horrified by the crisis and, as he wrote in his diary,

> considering all aspects of the situation more harm than good would be done with any attempt to force conscription at this time. I could not bring myself to being the head of a Government which would take that course — a course which might, after five years of war in Europe . . . lead to spurts of civil war in our own country. It would be a criminal thing, and would destroy the entire War record.

Caricature of King by Robert LaPalme.

"BRAVE MEN SHALL NOT DIE BECAUSE *I* FALTERED"

What can *I do?*

THERE is one job you *alone* can do. It concerns the man you love. He has a terrific task ahead of him—a task that will get more irksome as the days go by, until this war is won—or until we shall lie vanquished at Hitler's feet.

So we ask you to help him keep fit and happy for his job, whether it be on the production line or the firing line; in the factory or in the office; producing munitions of war or maintaining essential war services.

More and more will be expected of him as the days go on. He will be tired . . . at times depressed with the seemingly endless cry for more and still more of his time and energy.

Be thoughtful of him. When he spends more hours at his desk or with his tools than in the past, he is not being intentionally neglectful of you. Those evenings you have enjoyed at the movies or at social gatherings may become fewer and fewer, because his hours of sleep are so important to him and to those who are dependent on him for supplies.

Make it your duty to keep him fit and happy for his job. Be sympathetic, patient and understanding when he is tired and fretful. Encourage him in his sacrifice by showing your pride in his achievements. Give him the happy smile when problems you may not be able to share cast their shadow across his face.

This is the responsibility of every woman who cherishes the love of a man and deserves his esteem.

This message is issued by the Department of Munitions and Supply for Canada

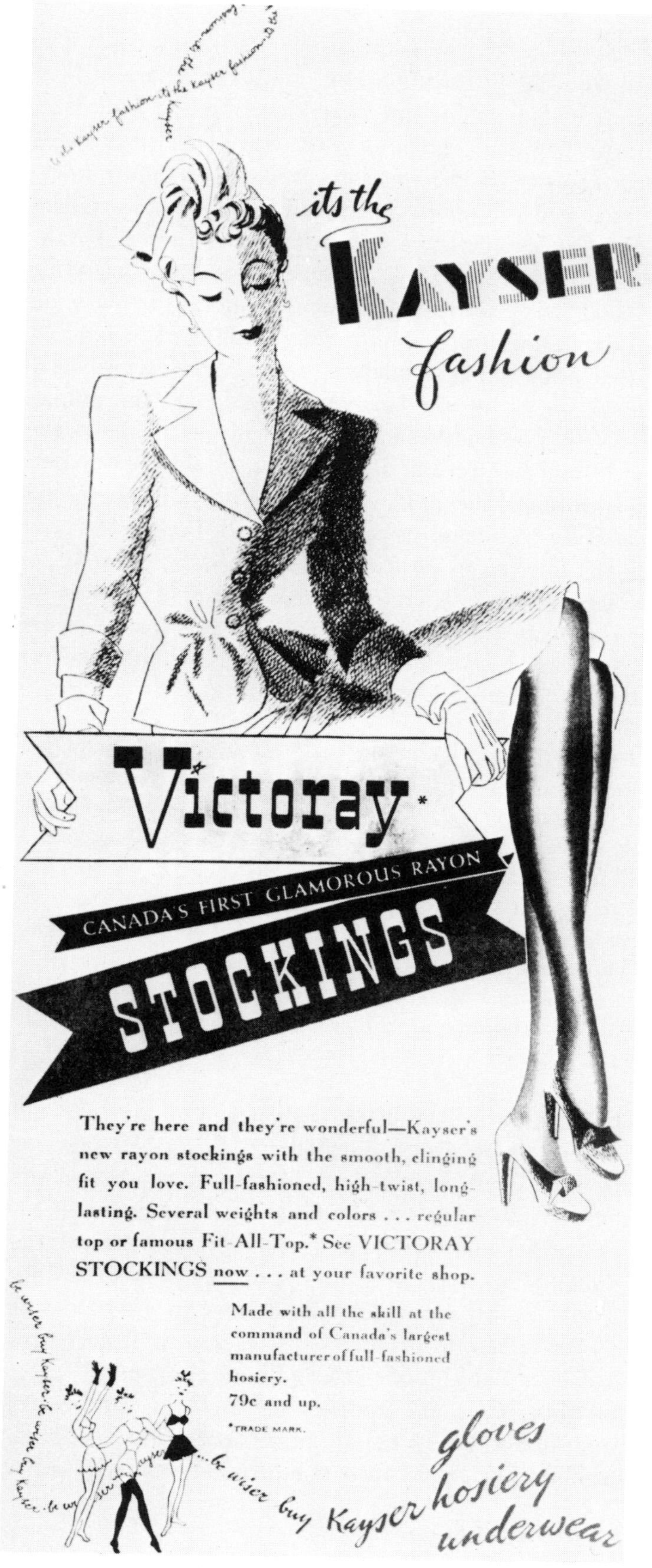
its the Kayser fashion
its the
KAYSER
fashion
Victoray*
CANADA'S FIRST GLAMOROUS RAYON
STOCKINGS
They're here and they're wonderful—Kayser's new rayon stockings with the smooth, clinging fit you love. Full-fashioned, high-twist, long-lasting. Several weights and colors . . . regular top or famous Fit-All-Top.* See VICTORAY STOCKINGS now . . . at your favorite shop.
Made with all the skill at the command of Canada's largest manufacturer of full-fashioned hosiery.
79c and up.
*TRADE MARK.
... be wiser buy Kayser
gloves
hosiery
underwear

OPPOSITE Wartime ad from *Chatelaine*, 1942. *Metropolitan Toronto Library Board.*

LEFT The '40s style, from *Chatelaine*, 1942. *Metropolitan Toronto Library Board.*

The Prime Minister had made up his mind. He remained firm throughout the long cabinet meetings that searched for a way out of the government's dilemma at the end of October 1944. For almost two weeks the ministers wrestled with the question and analyzed the confusing data. Positions finally polarized: all the Quebec ministers and many of the English-speaking ones supported King's anti-conscription policy, while several stood with Ralston and conscription. But Ralston remained the key figure, stubborn, tenacious, hard to fight.

At this point King's thoughts turned to General McNaughton. Immensely popular overseas and with the public, Andy McNaughton had been relieved of his command at the end of 1943 and had returned to Canada, ostensibly for reasons of health but in fact because British officers felt he could not successfully command troops in the field. Perhaps he now could be the answer to Mackenzie King's difficulties. If he could replace Ralston, King pondered, he might be able to persuade the NRMA troops to volunteer and thus spare Canada a terrible crisis. The ambitious General was willing, and on November 1 Mackenzie King faced his cabinet:

> I then said I thought we ought to, if possible, reach a conclusion without further delay. . . . I realized some way would have to be found . . . to save the government and to save a terrible division at this time. . . . That I had been asking myself was there anyone who could do this. . . . If there was, I thought it was owing to the country that such a person's services should be secured. I said I believed I had the man who could undertake that task and carry it out. I then mentioned General McNaughton's name. . . . I said that he believed he could get the reinforcements that were necessary . . .

If McNaughton came in, Ralston went out. The Minister, old and tired beyond his years, worn down by his labours for the troops, rose from the cabinet table, shook hands and left the Council chamber for the last time. The remainder of his colleagues sat shaken, while King said, "It was one of the hardest things I had to do in my life, but that it was the only course I could see for me which would serve to meet the war situation." At least one of the ministers saw it differently: "This is the most cold-blooded thing I have ever seen."

Unfortunately, it was not successful. McNaughton had been a good soldier, but he could not succeed at the task King had given him. The NRMA men would not be moved, either by appeals to their patriotism or by threats. The Army officers tried to persuade them and failed, and the result after some three weeks came in a memorandum from the military chiefs to McNaughton that stated baldly that the voluntary system had collapsed and that the NRMA men would have to be conscripted. For the new Minister of National Defence, this was "a blow in the stomach," and he somehow conveyed to the Prime Minister the feeling that the military machine had broken down. To King, realizing that the conscriptionist ministers in his cabinet were likely to walk out at any minute, McNaughton's terrible advice came at just the right psychological moment:

> It was apparent to me that to whatever bad management this may have been due, we are faced with a real situation which has to be met and now there is no longer thought as to the nature of the military advice tendered, particularly by General McNaughton . . . it will be my clear duty to agree to the passing of the order in council [authorizing the sending of NRMA troops overseas] and go to Parliament and ask for a vote of confidence. . . . This really lifts an enormous burden from my mind as after yesterday's Council it was apparent to me that it was only a matter of days before there would be no Government in Canada and this in the middle of war with our men giving their lives at the front.

Mackenzie King's decision for conscription had been taken.

Hurried consultations with key ministers followed, most notably with St. Laurent, reluctantly persuaded to support the Prime Minister by the threat of military resignations. A stunned cabinet, many of its ministers having come with their resignations ready in their pockets, heard Mackenzie King reverse his position and agree to conscription. Chubby Power, an able man who remembered his anti-conscriptionist pledges to his electors and who believed that conscription would have divisive effects, resigned, but everyone else stayed in the government. The Quebec backbench Members were now the key factor, but King delivered the speech of his life to them in the House on November 27 and persuaded them to stay with him. He quoted an address that Laurier had made on March 13, 1900:

> If there is anything to which I have devoted my political life, it is to try to promote unity, harmony and amity between the diverse elements of this country. My friends can

Armistice Day, Toronto, by George Agnew Reid.
Acc. No. 8685, Canadian War Museum, National Museum of Man, National Museums Canada.
An artist's record of the nation's sudden release from tension when World War I ended on November 11, 1918.

The VE-Day Parade on Sparks Street, in Ottawa.
Public Archives Canada, Z-3848-28.

The VE-Day celebrations
on Parliament Hill, May
8, 1945.
*Public Archives Canada,
Z-3849-17.*

desert me, they can remove their confidence from me, they can withdraw the trust they have placed in my hands; but never shall I deviate from that line of policy. Whatever may be the consequences, whether loss of prestige, loss of popularity or loss of power, I feel that I am in the right, and I know that a time will come when every man will render me full justice on that score.

Delivered with his back to the Opposition in the Commons chamber and facing his own supporters, it was one of the great moments of Parliament. The heir of Laurier put his career on the line, and French Canada's representatives supported him.

In the end just 15,000 or so NRMA men went overseas and only 2463 of them found their way to fighting units in North West Europe before the German surrender on May 8, 1945. By all reports the conscripts acquitted themselves like other soldiers, fighting and dying much as the volunteers did. Certainly enough Canadians fought and died in the war. Approximately one million served in the three services, about one-tenth of the total population. Of those, 2204 died in the Royal Canadian Navy's gallant struggles in the Atlantic and elsewhere, 17,101 were killed while serving in the Royal Canadian Air Force, and 22,917 died in the Canadian Army's battles in Hong Kong, at Dieppe, in Italy, and in northwest Europe. The price for the follies of European diplomacy had been high — over 40,000 dead — and hundreds and thousands more would bear wounds and injuries and scars for the rest of their days.

The war effort of Canada had been magnificent, unstinting on land, sea, and air, unequalled in factories and fields. It was an effort that made Canada a great industrial power and one of the world's leading nations for a brief period of time. Millions of Canadians had made it so, and they all deserve the credit. So too does Mackenzie King, who led the government during this critical period, who brought a united country into the war and a united country out of it.

After the conscription crisis, King reflected on his role:

> Certainly I shall never have another task comparable to the one of the past six weeks. Over and over again I have thought . . . that some day the world will know some of the things that I have prevented. I doubt if they will ever know what has been prevented at this time. I must make increasingly clear to the world that prevention of wrong courses of evil and the like means more than all else that man can accomplish. That lesson surely should be the one that comes out of the war.

King's creed was not an inspiring one, but he had prevented some drastic events during the conscription crisis. The breakup of the government and the Liberal party was one; the prevention of a divisive wartime election another; and widespread resignations from the cabinet yet a third. Equally important, he had kept the army overseas fully maintained and he had not permitted an irreparable breach between English and French Canadians to occur. All were important and critical: they form a record that entitles King to a high place among Canadian Prime Ministers. When one adds to these achievements his record of wartime social legislation, his record is indeed a good one.

Laurier House, bequeathed to Mackenzie King
by Lady Laurier, who died shortly after he
was elected leader of the Liberal Party in
1921. Well-to-do friends completely renovated
the building before King moved in. The
exterior was little changed, but the simple
rooms of Laurier's time gave way to an
elaborately luxurious interior.
Parks Canada.

7

A Brave New World

"I HAVE BEEN THINKING a good deal in the last 48 hours about the future," Mackenzie King wrote in his diary early in January 1943. After a conversation with Ian Mackenzie, the Minister of Pensions and Health, he recorded that the minister had

> said to me that he thought what should be done, what he would like to see done and what he believes the party would like and be best for the country would be for me to lead the party through another general election. To make the post-war program of social reform and the peace conference, the main subject of appeal. That it would be a natural rounding out of my life-work . . . old age pensions; unemployment insurance, etc. . . . In other words, make a complete programme of social security. My whole record of public life would back up the sincerity of my appeal. . . . I agreed with him that nothing could more completely please me if I had the physical strength and endurance . . .

That conversation with Mackenzie, a shrewd political tactician, was an important one in shaping the policy of the Prime Minister for the rest of the war years. It laid out the issues on which he would fight the election of 1945 — social security and peace — and it did press King on to what he saw as the rounding out of his life's work.

The 1919 Liberal platform, largely drafted in its social welfare sections by King, had laid out an impressive program for the future. Little of it had been enacted by King, despite his long years in power. Old-age pensions had come in the 1920s, but in a very ungenerous form and only with a means test. Unemployment insurance had finally become law in

1940, but only after the worst of the Depression had passed and after the war had begun to create thousands of new jobs in and out of uniform. But people had no financial protection against sickness, families no assistance to help them raise their offspring. Most people still held the attitude that social welfare was best left to private charity rather than to governments; not even the suffering of the Depression had really altered that sentiment. In addition, constitutional difficulties faced the federal government if it tried to move into jurisdictional areas given by the British North America Act to the provinces. The long struggle for unemployment insurance showed this difficulty, and the report of the Royal Commission on Dominion-Provincial Relations, released in 1940, met with sharp criticism from Ontario, Alberta, and British Columbia, in part because of their worry about erosion of their powers, a concern that effectively blocked any effective action at a Dominion-Provincial conference in January 1941.

The war began to change all this, however. The long struggle, the many sacrifices demanded from the people, and the expectations of a better world after the peace all combined to produce radical changes. One such alteration came in the political arena where the Cooperative Commonwealth Federation began to increase its support substantially. In British Columbia in the fall of 1941, the CCF became the Opposition, strong enough to drive the Liberals and Conservatives into coalition, and in the York South by-election the next year

Mackenzie King with the premiers of the provinces at the abortive Dominion-Provincial Conference held in Ottawa as the war was ending, in August 1945. Left to right: Hon. E. C. Manning (Alberta), Hon. J. W. Jones (Prince Edward Island), Hon. S. S. Garson (Manitoba), Hon. A. S. MacMillan (Nova Scotia), Hon. G. A. Drew (Ontario), Mr. King, Hon. M. L. Duplessis (Quebec), Hon. J. B. McNair (New Brunswick), Hon. John Hart (British Columbia), and Hon. T. C. Douglas (Saskatchewan).
Public Archives Canada,
C-26935.

the party had achieved national notice by destroying the comeback attempt of Arthur Meighen. Soon party membership began to expand rapidly and funds became available in large quantities. The CCF capitalized on its new strength by winning two federal by-elections in August 1943 and by soaring dramatically from zero to 34 seats in the Ontario provincial elections in the same month; the Gallup Polls of September 1943, in fact, showed the socialist party with 29 per cent of the public's support in Canada, a single point ahead of both the Liberals and the Conservatives. This extraordinary shift in political sentiment seemed based on fear — fear that the Depression would resume once the war ended, fear that the old parties could not manage a peacetime economy, fear that social-welfare legislation would never be implemented by a government committed to free enterprise.

The old parties uncomfortably watched this shift in public feeling, and the Conservatives were the first to react to it. Meighen's defeat by the CCF had shaken the old Tory party and many feared for its life. The response came in the summer of 1942 when a group of younger and more progressive Conservatives called a conference at Port Hope, Ontario, and produced a draft platform for their party, a platform that called for the recognition of labour's rights to collective bargaining, for family allowances, medicare, health insurance, and a host of social-welfare measures. Some Tories scoffed, but at a party leadership convention in Winnipeg in December 1942, the "Port Hopefuls" platform was adopted virtually intact. Even more important, the party chose as its leader John Bracken, the longtime Premier of Manitoba and a man who had never had connections with the party. Bracken was an old Progressive who had demonstrated a unique ability to swallow up the opposition in his province so that sometimes he was a Liberal-Progressive and sometimes he was not. Now he hoped to transfer this ability to the Conservative party whose name, at his insistence, was changed to Progressive Conservative. Wags jeered at the Pro and Con party, but clearly Conservatism was making a pitch to hold the centre of the political road on the philosophy, stated frankly by one of the leaders of the Port Hopefuls, that half a loaf was better than none.

Only the government was slow to react to the changed political reality. King and his key ministers spent all their waking hours dealing with the crises of the moment and running the war effort, a massive, formidable task. The civil serv-

Mackenzie King and
Louis St. Laurent, then
Minister of Justice, broad-
casting to the Canadian
people on VE-Day —
May 8, 1945 — from San
Francisco, where they
were attending the found-
ing conference of the
United Nations.
*Public Archives Canada,
C-22716.*

ice, usually the source of fertile ideas, was similarly over-
worked. But ideas were percolating toward the top and most
were coming from within Ian Mackenzie's Pensions department and from committees responsible to it.

One such was the Committee on Reconstruction, an ad-
visory body formed in March 1941 and headed by the Principal of McGill University, F. Cyril James. The James
Committee had launched a series of wideranging studies soon
after its creation that explored the impact peace would have
on Canadian society and the economy. The Committee's
initial conclusions were somber: "If, for any reason, reconstruction should not proceed smoothly during the postwar
recession the country would inevitably be confronted by
rapidly mounting unemployment and widespread dissatisfac-
tion." How could this resumption of the Depression be
avoided? That question concerned everyone, and the best
answer seemed to lie in the application of Keynesian economics, that pump-priming philosophy that the King government had hesitantly adopted just before the war.

Keynesianism motivated the thinking behind the most
important product of the Committee on Reconstruction. This
was the so-called Marsh Report, *The Report on Social Security
for Canada*, prepared by the Committee's research director,

A corner of the book-lined study on the third floor of Laurier House. It has been called the room from which Canada was governed for more than two decades. A prominent feature was the portrait of his mother, lighted night and day by a special lamp.
Laurier House,
Public Archives Canada.

Dr. L. C. Marsh, and released in March 1943. Marsh argued effectively that social security had to be the responsibility of the community as a whole and that it had to include protection against unemployment, sickness, and old age. And, he argued, "One of the necessities for economic stability is the maintenance of the flow of purchasing power at the time when munitions and other factories are closing down. . . . In this perspective, a wide and properly integrated scheme of social insurance and welfare provision of $100,000,000 or $500,-000,000 is not to be regarded with the alarm which . . . it might otherwise occasion." What Marsh argued, in sum, was that the economy could be kept going after the war by putting money into people's hands through welfare payments, a radical thought indeed and one that upset editorial writers and the Prime Minister.

Not that King disagreed with the thrust of Marsh's proposals, suggestions that included family allowances and the provision of "a national minimum" to Canadians. They were all part of the 1919 program, all part of King's book on *Industry and Humanity* written a quarter-century before. But where would the money come from? How could he bribe the people with their own money? This quandary upset the Prime Minister, and he told his party caucus, "I would never allow an appeal to the people on social security measures at a time of war with a view to bringing them to support the government because of what it would pay out of the public treasury." It all went against King's grain. "It was wrong," he said, "to think of increased outlays on anything that could be avoided until victory was won. Important, however, to keep everything in readiness for the peace." That last sentence justified continued planning and eventually after the Liberal defeat in the provincial election in Ontario and in the federal by-elections in August 1943, King came to believe that more would have to be done now.

The upshot was the first meeting of the National Liberal Federation since the outbreak of war. In September 1943,

Mackenzie King and Louis St. Laurent, then Minister of Justice, at the founding conference of the United Nations in San Francisco, April-June 1945.
Public Archives Canada, C-22717.

the party gathered at the Chateau Laurier in Ottawa to draw up its own platform. The Liberal program, like the CCF's, like the Conservatives', set out on the new road to the welfare state. Promises for full employment, for social security, for a rising standard of living were made, as well as support for "both public and private enterprise." The Liberal party had now fixed its direction and, unlike the CCF and the PCs, it had one great advantage: it held power and could implement its pledges.

This it began to do, giving notice of its intent in the Speech from the Throne that opened the 1944 session of Parliament on January 27. "The post-war object of our domestic policy is social security and human welfare," the Governor General intoned. "The establishment of a national minimum of social security and human welfare should be advanced as rapidly as possible." To this end, the government indicated that its planning for the peace concentrated on three areas: the demobilization, rehabilitation, and re-establishment of veterans, the conversion of the economy from war to peace, and social security. New departments of government were established to administer these areas. Equally important, the government pledged that it would introduce family allowances, seek the agreement of the provinces for health insurance, and reorganize and increase old-age pensions. Health insurance would unfortunately be delayed for two decades, as would efforts to create a national contributory old-age pension scheme, but family allowances soon became law.

The family allowance bill on its own amounted to something in the nature of a social revolution. Marsh had demonstrated in his report that millions of Canadians could not make ends meet and that as a result their children were suffering in health and opportunity. This lack had to be an important concern for any government. Equally so was the wartime consideration that by paying an allowance to families with children, the effective wages of a worker could be increased to meet a family's needs without destroying the government's wage-control policies. Most important of all, a memorandum to Mackenzie King and the cabinet pointed out, "The economic problem after the war will not be to produce what we need, but to find markets for what we must produce if we are to avoid unemployment. The provision of children's allowances would almost certainly result in a considerable net addition to the home market both for food and manufactured goods." Anything that promised increased public spending after the war was good, or so the economists now believed.

Strangely, Mackenzie King initially was blind to this argument. He told his ministers at one point that "to tell the country that everyone was to get a family allowance was sheer folly; it would occasion great resentment everywhere. Great care," he maintained, "had to be taken in any monies given out from the Treasury as distinguished from exempting portions of income already earned." But when King talked with one of his assistants, a supporter of family allowances, and learned that this young man had been educated because of a Great War widow's pension paid to his mother, he suddenly realized that in principle that pension differed little from family allowances. Both, he now saw, could help bright young people to get a chance. Converted, his task was now to persuade the cabinet, caucus, Parliament, and the people.

The cabinet decision effectively took place on January 13, 1944, when King argued passionately, "I thought the Creator intended that all persons born should have equal opportunities. Equal opportunity started in days of infancy and the first thing, at least, was to see that the children got the essentials of life . . ." Some ministers disagreed, but cabinet as a whole approved. Caucus also soon came to support the measure, and the Family Allowance bill was introduced into Parliament in the summer of 1944. Under its terms, the family of a child under 5 years of age would receive $5 a month, $6 for those from 6 to 9 years, $7 for those from 10 to 12, and $8 for children to 15. Those figures today sound inconsequential, but at a period when a good wage was $30 a week, they amounted to a substantial infusion of cash into family budgets.

So powerful was this political package that the House of Commons approved it on second reading without a dissenting vote, almost unheard of. But there was opposition to the measure. To one Toronto MP (who absented himself from the House when the vote was taken) the bill would lead to federal funds being used in "bonussing families who have been unwilling to defend their country," a direct attack at Quebec, its higher birth rate, and its unwillingness to countenance conscription. John Bracken, the PC leader who had no seat in Parliament as yet, called the bill a "political bribe" directed at French Canada, and a Conservative social critic feared that the extra money would encourage large families among the "erratic, irresponsible, bewildered of mind, and socially incapable, feeble-minded and mentally affected . . ."

OPPOSITE King in the book-lined study on the third floor of Laurier House. It has been called the room from which Canada was governed for more than two decades.
Photo by Roger Coster copyright © Life Magazine, New York, N.Y.; Public Archives Canada, C-1775.

Not all Conservatives felt this way, and such men as the Member of Parliament for Lake Centre, Sask., John Diefenbaker, crusaded hard in caucus for family allowances. But the net result of Conservative criticisms was twofold: Quebec became ever more convinced that it had few friends in the Progressive Conservative party; and the public in Canada as a whole began to reach the conclusion that the Port Hope and Winnipeg platforms were just words.

Family allowances would cost the taxpayer between $200 and $250 million a year, a sum that came close to being half the entire pre-war federal budget. This was Keynesianism with a vengeance, and it was not the only federal measure of its kind. Unemployment insurance, established at the beginning of the war, had $250 million accumulated and ready to help fight privation among those who might lose their jobs with the peace. The National Housing Act aimed to spur $1 billion in new construction and Ottawa would contribute $275 million to this end. The public appropriation to maintain floor prices in agriculture and fishing amounted to $225 million, and the war-service gratuities to be given Canada's veterans, a well thought out and generous scheme, would amount to some $1.2 billion and would include clothing, education, land-settlement grants, and the like. All in all, Ottawa was prepared to pour more than $3 billion into the postwar economy in an effort to maintain purchasing power and keep industry moving. It really was true, as one Liberal cabinet minister told a ccf friend, "You socialists have schemes, but I have the bills right here in my pocket."

That comment illustrated the political dimensions of the King government's policies. The ccf seemed to be the threat, and the great social welfare bills were conservative measures designed to halt the growth of the socialist party. But after the conscription crisis of 1944, after English-Canadian opinion was aroused at the government's hesitancy, and after French-Canadian opinion was angered by the government's eventual move to the draft, everything political seemed up in the air. Every wartime government has to do unpleasant acts, and traditionally wartime governments have paid the price at the polls. But in 1945 it did not seem so clear.

To many Canadians, the ccf seemed radical and dangerous. The socialist party was perceived as the captive of organized labour, one element in society that had made enormous gains during the war in establishing its right to exist, its right to collective bargaining, and its right to represent the workers of Canada. The link between labour and the CCF frightened business executives and many ordinary citizens who were helped to reach their judgments by a skillful and lavishly financed propaganda campaign mounted by a number of anti-socialist organizations, well financed by banks and large industrial concerns. Full page advertisements in the press lambasted the CCF, claiming that if the party were elected it would substitute "a foreign-born scheme of State Socialism for our democratic way of life." CCF politicians wanted "complete control of our lives" so they could impose "absolute dictatorship" and make Canadians into "animals in a zoo." There was much more in the same vein, mixed with attacks on some CCF leaders and particularly on party organizer David Lewis whose Jewish and Russian origins were repeatedly noted: "The day may yet come in Canada when a Jewish immigrant boy, whose father saw fit to forsake the Bolshevik Communist atmosphere of Russia, will rise to a position where he writes the ticket for the social and economic program of this nation . . ." Not even the good record rapidly built up in Saskatchewan, where the CCF had won power in 1944, could counter the impressions created by these scare tactics.

The Conservatives, too, had liabilities in the public eye. The party had no support in Quebec, and Bracken had not established a clear image of himself, not even in his native West. Many feared that a Conservative government would be against welfare measures, and many remembered the Tories, rather unfairly, as the Depression party. This process of elimination left only the Liberals. Mackenzie King had his liabilities, everyone knew. He was not an inspiring leader, he was devious, tricky, and too subservient to Quebec, or so thought many in English Canada. To Quebec, he had betrayed his pledges in 1942 and 1944, and he seemed just an English-Canadian politician like the others.

But Mackenzie King did seem to be the best of a bad lot. Who else, after all, could Quebec vote for? Not the Tories. Not the socialist CCF whose doctrines were rejected by the Church. There was the *Bloc Populaire Canadien*, a nationalist party that had been formed after the success of the *Ligue pour la défense du Canada* in the plebiscite campaign, but the *Bloc* was divided, dissension-ridden, and it had no chance of forming the government. Who else was there but Mackenzie King? In English Canada, calculations were not dissimilar. King had run a good war effort, people were prosperous, and the social-welfare state was now almost a reality. Mackenzie King probably did seem the best choice to make the peace.

This line shaped King's election campaign in April and May 1945, much as he and Ian Mackenzie had discussed in January 1943. In his first national radio address, King appealed "for a renewed expression of your confidence . . . in terms not of promise, but of performance." The people would have to decide either to allow "the affairs of our country in its national and international relations" to be carried on by the "tried and trusted administration which you know" or handed over "to unknown and untried hands." King was the man for making the peace; he was also the man to further the social welfare state:

> My life's interests, I need not tell you, have been with the cause of peace and with the promotion of human welfare and social reform. It is because I see, close at hand, unparalleled opportunities to further these great ends that I should like to serve in another Parliament.

Against this Bracken and the Conservatives foolishly tried to fight the election on conscription. The government had messed up the manpower question, they argued, and if elected they would send conscripts to fight the war against Japan still raging in the Pacific. Unhappily for the Tories, the Pacific war rightly or wrongly interested almost no one in Canada; conscription, after the German surrender, was no longer a winning issue. Bracken preached only to the converted and to the problems of the past. "Remember," the Prime Minister countered, "from now on, it is with the future, not with the past, that you should be concerned." People remembered.

The result of the election was another Mackenzie King victory, but a narrow one. The Liberals captured 127 seats in the House of Commons of 245, while the Conservatives took 67 and the CCF 28. Quebec became the key, giving the Liberals 53 seats and half the popular vote, a tribute to King's policies but also a reflection of the absence of choice for the *Québécois*. In Ontario, King won 34 seats to Bracken's 48, while the CCF, despite polling a quarter of a million votes, failed to elect a single MP. In the West the Liberals lost 25 of the 44 seats they had won in 1940, most to the CCF, and in the Maritimes the balance remained the same as five years earlier.

Mackenzie King lost his own seat in Prince Albert, Sask., a casualty of the last counted servicemen's vote. But still he was relieved by the party's victory, by his last election victory:

I sat quietly for a time in the sunroom, in my heart thanking and praising God for his goodness. The relief of mind that I experience is indescribable. It brings with it peace of heart as well . . . almost as if I had a bath after a dusty and dirty journey, with the storm of lies, misrepresentations, insinuations and what not in which I have had to pass during the past few weeks — I might even say over most of the years of the war. One could go back and say almost over one's public life. I felt a real vindication in the verdict of the people and the sense of triumph therefrom.

His sense of triumph was justified. Few wartime governments survived among the Allies, and even Winston Churchill, Britain's saviour, was ignominiously routed at the polls by an ungrateful nation at much the same time that Mackenzie King savoured his victory.

Mackenzie King riding with Field Marshal Jan Smuts, Prime Minister of South Africa, in the Victory Parade in London on June 8, 1946.
Public Archives Canada, C-9279.

Perhaps one reason that Mackenzie King had been returned in the election of 1945 was the sense of nationalism that the war had produced in Canada, a sense of security engendered by the state's increased role in ensuring a minimum standard for its people, and a sense of increased importance that the war had given Canadians about their place in the world. Part was attributable to the military effort — Canada had the fourth largest air force, for instance — and part to the extraordinary productivity of the nation's farms and factories. Part sprang from Canadian pride at being a donor of aid, and not, as almost every other Ally, a recipient.

The war had altered Canada's place in the world. Before the war, the nation had been virtually a colony in every way that mattered. The war made Canada into a middle power, an ill-defined status but one certainly different from the position in 1939. Canada was not a giant in military terms or in world

Mrs. Patteson, King's friend, companion, and confidante.
Public Archives Canada, C-14174.

Mackenzie King's country retreat at Kingsmere, where he died on July 22, 1950. The Kingsmere estate, comprising some 500 acres, was assembled over a long period. The name was not a reference to King himself; Kingsmere, the small lake after which the community was called, was named long before Mr. King owned any property there. *Public Archives Canada, C-80153.*

influence, although in some areas — the production of food, the extraction of minerals, and in the potential for civil air transport — it had virtually great-power status. This realization during the war, coupled with a building resentment at the way the Great Powers ignored Canada when it suited their interests, led to the development of the "functional principle," probably the first independently derived Canadian position in international politics. The principle of functionalism developed within the Department of External Affairs in 1942 as Canada fought and argued for inclusion on the series of Combined Boards established by Britain and the United States to coordinate the war effort. The Dominion had scant success initially, although in due course Canada would win a place on the Combined Food Board and on the Combined Production and Resources Board. This difficult experience crystallized thinking and led to Mackenzie King's clear statement of functionalism in July 1943:

King in the role of gentleman farmer, with the sheep that were briefly a feature of his Kingsmere estate. He found that they fell victims to dogs and disease and soon disposed of them.
Public Archives Canada, C-9051.

. . . authority in international affairs must not be concentrated exclusively in the largest powers. . . . A number of new international organizations are likely to be set up as a result of the war. In the view of the government, effective representation on these bodies should neither be restricted to the largest states nor necessarily extended to all states. Representation should be determined on a functional basis which will admit to full membership those countries, large or small, which have the greatest contribution to make to the particular object in question.

In other words, where Canada had the capacity to act as a great power, it should be so treated.

Unfortunately, this principle never did win ready acceptance. Canada remained outside the major decision-making bodies and never pressed as forthrightly as it might have to win entry. But recognition had to be accorded the Dominion's monetary and productive power, and Canada did secure a place in the higher councils of the United Nations Relief and Rehabilitation Administration, the great organization set up to administer relief aid to the war-torn countries. But at the creation of the United Nations Organization at the San Francisco Conference in the spring of 1945, Canada again failed to see its middle-power status protected in the Charter, although in practical terms a kind of recognition was accorded to it and to other similar-sized states. The postwar world was going to be run by the Great Powers, but Canada would be an important adjunct to them.

"How important" was a question that concerned Ottawa. During the war, the British time and again had tried to lump Canada and the other Dominions into a Commonwealth bloc, directed and run from Whitehall. This tactic had been objected to by Mackenzie King since Chanak in 1922, and one might reasonably have expected that London had got the message after two decades. But Prime Minister Churchill tried to structure a role in the emerging United Nations for an Empire bloc, and the Ambassador in Washington, Lord Halifax, even spoke in Toronto in January 1944 in support of a world of "titans," with Britain and its Commonwealth as one of these giants. To Mackenzie King, nothing of the kind could be tolerated. His response to Halifax was a calmly delivered but pointed rejection and, at a Commonwealth Prime Ministers' meeting in London in May 1944, he finally laid the united Empire to rest once and forever. Canada stayed happily in the Commonwealth and the war had made individual ties to Britons closer than ever, but in terms of policy in the world, Canada would now be independent.

Still, the country was too close to one of the Great Powers for comfort. The war had forced Canada and the United States into close economic and military cooperation and the economies of the two became virtually intertwined. The war also created a dearth of British capital investment in Canada and increased the opportunities for American investors, a chance they did not neglect. In addition, because of the Japanese threat to the North Pacific coast in 1942 and 1943, Alaska assumed a position of critical importance in North American defence, a condition that led to far-reaching developments. The Alaska Highway was pushed through the North, its construction being run by the United States Army. The CANOL project, a scheme to ship oil from Norman Wells, N.W.T., north into Alaska was completed at high cost. And a network of airfields was built to facilitate the flow of fighters and supplies into the North. The enormous expenditures opened the North in a way that few had dreamed possible,

and this development was good for the country. But the Americans, anxious about Alaska, began to pour troops and supplies into Canada, and the new presence was not always tactfully handled. Some Canadians and Americans began to refer jokingly to the American "army of occupation" in Canada; undoubtedly, Ottawa was lax in watching over Dominion sovereignty. By 1943, the government had moved to hold its own, and great care was taken to ensure that the Americans left with the peace and that their installations were purchased from them.

By the end of the war, however, Canada's geographic nearness to the Soviet Union had become a concern, one that also affected relations with Washington. Even before the war in Europe had been won, Canadian planners foresaw eventual difficulties with the Soviet Union, and they expected, as a paper accepted by the cabinet indicated, that the United States would "take an active interest in Canadian defence preparations in the future" simply because "Canada lies astride the overland route between the United States and the USSR." Any deterioration in American relations with Russia would be embarrassing to Canada, the planners noted, but it was very clear that in the event of any such embarrassment Canada would stand firmly with the United States.

As the wartime alliance quickly began to collapse with the peace and as bitter disputes followed in the United Nations and in Great Power meetings, the question of Canada's relations with the Soviet Union became of some importance. Canada had exchanged diplomatic representatives with Moscow during the war, and the Russians maintained a large establishment in Ottawa. People often wondered idly what all the Soviet diplomats were doing, and on September 6, 1945, Canadians began to discover. That day, Igor Gouzenko, a cipher clerk in the Soviet Embassy, found his way to the Royal Canadian Mounted Police in Ottawa with documents and tales of a widespread Soviet spy ring operating in Canada. Gouzenko's revelations played an important part in beginning the Cold War with which we still live; more immediately they led to a secret order in council authorizing the Minister of Justice to jail suspected spies, without trial and without the normal protection of the law, and eventually to a Royal Commission. Among those found guilty of spying for the Russians was the private secretary to the British High Commissioner in Ottawa, a nuclear physicist, and a cipher clerk in the Department of External Affairs. Irrefutably, the spy ring

OPPOSITE Mackenzie King out for a stroll at Kingsmere with his dog, Pat, to which he was devoted. *Public Archives Canada, C-20049.*

had been directed from the Russian Embassy and had passed on information of great value.

The shock of this revelation was profound. Mackenzie King was stunned:

> I think of the Russian Embassy being only a few doors away and of there being there a centre of intrigue. During this period of war, while Canada has been helping Russia . . . there had been one branch of the Russian service that has been spying on all matters relating to location of American troops, atomic bombs, processes, etc. . . . All this helps to explain the Russian attitude . . . in blocking whatever seemed to stand in Russia's way to increase her power and world control.

World War II was barely won and already World War III seemed a possibility.

The events of the next few years did nothing to decrease this fear. Soviet pressure in Europe increased, and the Russians actively worked to extend their influence in Eastern and Central Europe as they strove to create a large buffer zone between Russia and Germany. The Czech government, trying to be democratic and neutralist, was toppled by local Communists in early 1948 and additional Communist probes ranged from France to Iran to China, where the corrupt Nationalist regime of Chiang Kai-shek was under severe pressure from the Communists. It seemed to be a world conspiracy, directed and controlled from Moscow, and the West, weary of war and anxious for peace, began to fear not an invasion of Western Europe but the possible election of Communist governments in Italy or France. The Communists seemed to have enormous moral force behind them, to be the wave of the future. People were frightened everywhere, and even a Royal Canadian Mounted Police publication in 1949 stated, straight-faced, "A convinced Communist is a man possessed. He is not amenable to argument or persuasion, or even coercion. Society must always be on guard against him, and each citizen must be prepared to combat his ideas wherever they crop up."

The moral fibre of the democracies had to be strengthened to resist the new supermen, and in this effort Canada played a major role. As early as August 1947, a senior official of the Department of External Affairs bemoaned the failure of the United Nations to preserve peace and called for the creation of a regional security pact among the nations of the North

Atlantic. Within months, talks were underway in Europe and Washington that led to the signing of the North Atlantic Treaty in 1949. At the same time, the United States established the Marshall Plan, a device to pour American goods into a Europe that could not pay for them. Canada developed a similar policy by giving a huge $1,250,000,000 loan to Britain in 1946 and lesser sums to other traditional trading partners. Western Europe had to recover its economic strength and maintain its anti-Communist system of government, and American and Canadian policy aimed at this end.

Mackenzie King's position through this period was cautious. He feared Communism, but he worried about Canada being committed to war once again through decisions reached elsewhere. His fears about national unity, his worries about conscription still existed, and with reason. The armed forces had proposed peacetime conscription in 1945, for example, and the developing Soviet challenge led to occasional renewed cries for it in the next few years. Quebec still seemed isolationist, and King correctly feared the effects of a new war. But by 1948 King was tired and worn out. The old leader had been Prime Minister for more than 21 years and head of the Liberal Party for 29 years. He was in his 74th year, and the strain of taking decisions and avoiding others had ground him under. In 1946 he had turned over the portfolio of Secretary of State for External Affairs to Louis St. Laurent, the Quebec lawyer who had come into the cabinet in 1941 and whom King already envisaged as his successor. A French Canadian, St. Laurent shared few of the fears of his compatriots — or his Prime Minister — about world involvement, and he remained a convinced anti-Communist. Under his lead, the Department of External Affairs played an active role, one largely shaped by his Under Secretary, Lester Pearson.

St. Laurent wanted Canada to lead from its position of strength. And indeed Canada was strong. The postwar depression that people had foreseen and feared during the war did not materialize, as the savings of Canadians fuelled a new and greater boom with the peace. The government skillfully maintained controls and carefully watched the country's foreign exchange position, but the upward trend was pronounced. The Gross National Product had more than doubled during the course of the war, reaching $11.8 billion in 1945. By 1948 it had increased by almost half again to $16.3 billion, and a state of permanent boom seemed in progress. Wages rose, consumer goods filled the stores and homes, and investment

Mackenzie King on the platform at the 1948 Liberal leadership convention which, to his great satisfaction, chose Louis S. St. Laurent as his successor.
Copyright © Standard Photo; Public Archives Canada, C-31319.

in capital industries increased dramatically. The war had changed Canada into a major industrial power, a rich one, and times were good.

The events of the war also brought Confederation to completion. The island of Newfoundland had once been a Dominion, but the economic collapse of the Depression had forced the island to its knees and to a reversion to colonial status under an appointed commission government. The war had seen Canada and the United States station troops, aircraft, and ships in the area and occasionally jostle for influence, and with the peace Newfoundland's status had to be settled. Would the island become a Dominion once more or join with Canada as its tenth province? The debates were furious and prolonged, but the Canadian cause was championed by a remarkable man, Joey Smallwood, and it eventually triumphed narrowly. Engineering Newfoundland's accession to Canada was Mackenzie King's last triumph, although the formal papers would not be signed until after he had left office.

For Mackenzie King, it was finally time to go. His

health was breaking down, and he told one of his ministers that he was "a sick old dog." In January 1948 he finally took the plunge, informing the National Liberal Federation that a leadership convention should be summoned in August. As always he hedged his remarks enough so that he could stay on as Prime Minister, but this time King's qualifications and temporizing were sham. He was too old to hang on much longer and he knew it. The convention, a great affair, paid him tribute, cheered him to the echo, and chose as his successor Louis St. Laurent. With the cheers ringing in his ears, the old leader left the convention hall and entered the history books.

King would live only for two years more, dying on July 22, 1950, during another international crisis. The Korean War had begun and in the train on the way back from Mackenzie King's funeral, the cabinet decided that Canada should send troops to share in the United Nations' effort there. That decision effectively marked the end of the old era and the beginning of the new, for it was a decision that one can scarcely see Mackenzie King permitting. Canada had changed.

And Mackenzie King had led and shaped the changes. He had been Prime Minister through three distinct periods in our national history. He took power in the aftermath of a great war and found a nation economically weak and torn by dissension. His task was to restore unity, and he did to a substantial extent, consolidating his own power and that of the party he led as he did so. Then came the Depression when economics and foreign policy dominated affairs. King's task was to get the economy moving, something at which he did not really succeed, and to bring a united country into the war. This he accomplished. His third period of power saw him lead the country through the war and reconstruction, his period of greatest achievement. By supreme skill and judgment, he shaped a mighty war effort that kept Canadians together (as much as could be expected) and gave them incredible prosperity and power. For his achievements from 1940 to 1948, he should be honoured across the land.

But King is not remembered favourably by his compatriots, if he is remembered at all. His sexual proclivities, misinterpreted from the inconclusive evidence King left in his diaries, and his dealings with "the other world" have produced a figure of fun. The King diaries, one of the world's greatest documents, have helped to turn their author into a caricature of a frustrated mamma's boy, a secret practitioner of vice, a hypocrite. Worse, his perennial politics of compromise, of delay, of obfuscation obscure his real accomplishments, many of which are attributed to others. Only the blame for his failures is attached to Mackenzie King alone. This is unfair, of course, because King always had a difficult row to hoe, a divided, fractious country to govern. But govern it he did and he did it well. In the longer perspective, history will surely be more kind and Mackenzie King will rank with Macdonald and Laurier as the greatest of Canadian prime ministers.

Part of the famous ruins at Kingsmere. Ruins were not in King's mind when he acquired a handsome stone bay window from a building being demolished in Ottawa. He intended to incorporate it in a new study, but after the window had been put up at Kingsmere, the site was found unsuitable for a foundation. The abandoned window, crowning slope, had a picturesque and romantic air that appealed to King: he went on to gather the extraordinary collection of ruins that now stands on Kingsmere estate. Here, in his summer home, King died in 1950. *Parks Canada.*

Mackenzie King leaving
the leadership convention
at which his successor
Louis S. St. Laurent, had
been chosen — walking out
of politics and into history.
Public Archives Canada,
C-20621.

A Note on Sources

ONE OF THE BEST sources for the study of Mackenzie King's Canada is the King collection at the Public Archives of Canada. Mr. King kept everything, from Christmas cards to state documents, and the entire collection forms at once a political and social history of great importance. Particularly valuable are the King diaries, a massive, revealing guide to King's personality and to public policy. An edited version of the diary for the 1939 to 1948 period has been published as *The Mackenzie King Record*, edited by J. W. Pickersgill.

The official biography of Mackenzie King is complete to 1939. The first volume by R. M. Dawson and the second and third by H. Blair Neatby are fair and very competent assessments based on the King Papers and on a variety of other sources. The best popular biography of King is undoubtedly Bruce Hutchinson's *The Incredible Canadian*. Although published a quarter-century ago, this book is a sympathetic appraisal that still has genuine value for its insights and for its policy revelations. Charles Stacey's *A Very Double Life* (Toronto, 1976) looks at King's spiritualism, sex life, and finances.

There are also some biographies and studies of King's contemporaries. Vincent Massey, for a long period Canada's High Commissioner in London, has written an autobiography, and King's wartime Air Minister, Chubby Power, left a splendid memoir, aptly titled *A Party Politician*. Louis St. Laurent's life has been written by Dale Thomson. No serious studies have yet been done on C. D. Howe, J. L. Ilsley, or Colonel Ralston, and nothing on Lapointe or Dunning. General A. G. L. McNaughton is the subject of a three-volume study by John Swettenham, and the first volume of Lester Pearson's memoirs is very useful on the period to 1948.

For opposition politicians, there is similarly little. Arthur Meighen has been defended vigorously by Roger Graham in a very able three-volume biography, while no single adequate biography of R. B. Bennett is available, nor is anything as yet on John Bracken or George Drew. J. S. Woodsworth has been carefully studied by Kenneth McNaught in his fine biography, *A Prophet in Politics*, but there is nothing useful on Woodsworth's successors. There is a life entitled *Mitch Hepburn* by Neil McKenty and one entitled *Maurice Duplessis* by Conrad Black.

No general appraisal has been written of life in Canada in the 1920s, a decade that remains largely *terra incognita*. The best single source on the 1930s is Michiel Horn's documents collection, *The Dirty Thirties*. For World War II, the best source is Charles Stacey's massive official history, *Arms, Men and Governments: The War Policies of Canada 1939-1945*, while J. L. Granatstein's *Canada's War: The Politics of the Mackenzie King Government, 1939-1945* and his co-authored *Broken Promises: A History of Conscription in Canada* offer a somewhat different interpretation of many points.

In political party histories, most has been written about the CCF and Social Credit. For the CCF, Walter Young's *The Anatomy of a Party* is first class; on Social Credit, University of Toronto Press has published a large series under the general title of *Social Credit in Alberta*. Some of the volumes in this series, notably those by C. B. Macpherson and J. A. Irving, are very fine. Almost nothing has been written on the Liberal party, notwithstanding that party's hold on Canada for most of this century. On the Conservatives are two studies: J. R. Williams' sweeping look at the party from 1920 to 1949, and the more detailed examination of the party's trials during World War II by J. L. Granatstein.

For further sources, every reader should be aware of Claude Thibault, *Bibliographia Canadiana*, a huge guide to almost everything writen about Canada, or of J. L. Granatstein and P. D. Stevens, *Canada Since 1867: A Bibliographical Guide*.

Index

farmers, 28-30, 33-34
Ferguson, G. H., 41, 80
Fielding, W. S., 19ff., 39
Flavelle, Joseph, 27-28
Floud, Francis, 128
foreign investment, 72-74
foreign policy, 109ff., 184ff.
Forke, Robert, 42
Franco, Francisco, 124
free trade, 10, 14, 103-04
freight rates, 39
functionalism, 185-86

Gardiner, J. G., 30, 66, 104
general elections:
    1908: 10;
    1911: 10;
    1917: 12ff., 25;
    1921: 31ff.;
    1925: 41ff.;
    1926: 47ff.;
    1930: 79ff.;
    1935: 99ff.;
    1940: 144ff.;
    1945: 180ff.
generals' revolt, 163
Ginger Group, 41
Gladstone, W. E., 9
Godbout, A., 141
Gordon, Donald, 152
Gouin, Lomer, 39
Gouzenko, Igor, 189
Graham, G. P., 21ff., 39
group government, 28, 30
Group of Seven, 70, 115ff.

Halifax, Lord, 187
Hansen, Alvin, 104
Heaps, A. A., 44
Hepburn, Mitchell, 105-07, 145
Herridge, W. D., 117

Hitler, Adolf, 107, 120, 128, 129, 133
Hong Kong, 153
Houde, C., 148
Howe, C. D., 149
Hutterites, 67
Hyde Park Agreement, 150

Ilsley, J. L., 149
immigration, 42, 65ff.
Industry and Humanity, 21
Irvine, William, 30
isolationism, 68-69, 138

James, F. C., 172

Kai-shek, Chiang, 190
Kennedy, Leo, 71
Keynes, J. M., 104
Keynesianism, 174ff.
King, Isabel, 7
King, W. L. M., passim.:
    background, 7ff.;
    and sex, 7, 9;
    and convention 1919, 21ff.;
    Industry and Humanity, 21;
    and social reform, 21ff., 44, 168ff.;
    and French Canadians, 24;
    and Liberal reconciliation, 24ff.;
    and elections, 35ff., 41ff., 100ff., 144ff.,
        180ff.;
    and tariff, 35;
    and cabinet 1921, 37ff.;
    and constitutional crisis, 44ff.;
    and customs scandal, 45-46;
    and the Depression, 78ff.;
    and spiritualism, 80;
    Beauharnois affair, 91ff.;
    and foreign policy, 109ff., 184ff.;
    and U.K., 109ff.;
    at Imperial Conferences, 112, 113, 127, 187;